STOP GETTING
IN YOUR OWN WAY

STOP GETTING IN YOUR OWN WAY

A NO B.S GUIDE TO CREATING
THE BUSINESS OF YOUR DREAMS

JACLYN DIGREGORIO

NEW DEGREE PRESS

STOP GETTING IN YOUR OWN WAY

A No B.S Guide to Creating the Business of Your Dreams

ISBN   978-1-64137-332-6   *Paperback*

        978-1-64137-644-0   *Ebook*

CONTENTS

INTRODUCTION

———

MAY 7, 2017

Lying in my bed at 4:30 a.m., I felt wide awake and ready for the big day ahead. It was like I was six years old again, waiting to go downstairs to open presents from Santa Claus on Christmas morning.

I jumped out from under my covers and threw on my favorite yellow floral dress and a pair of blush pink Steve Madden sneakers. I quickly brushed my teeth and fixed my hair. Then, I put on a dab of blush, mascara, and pink lipstick. Finally, I was READY for the big day! I couldn't believe it was finally here.

I had been waiting for this day to come for so many months. I remember when I found out that it would take four to six months to produce and ship my plates. I was devastated that I would have to wait so long. As it often does, the time ended up going by faster than I imagined it would.

The delivery was scheduled for 11 a.m. I decided to have the boxes delivered to my grandmother's house so I could store them in her garage.

I arrived at 10:30 a.m., anxiously waiting for the driver to arrive. At one point, I was so nervous I almost threw up. It felt like the same anxiety I used to get before final exams in college.

When he pulled up, I was so happy that I began to tear up. In that moment, I knew what the rest of my life was going to look like. I was living out my purpose and chasing my dreams. I was exactly where I needed to be.

After unloading boxes for hours, all 450 sets of pineapple plates were stacked neatly in my grandmother's garage. I couldn't believe how many boxes there were. They took up the majority of the garage. I barely had any room to walk on either side of the boxes. Exhausted from the many trips I took between the garage and the truck, I finally found a small place to sit on the garage floor.

As I sat on the floor admiring the first product I ever created, I began to dream about the future. I created these pineapple plates to encourage young women to eat healthier, more balanced meals. Each part of the pineapple represented a different food group that is recommended in each meal.

I imagined selling my plates to college campuses across the country, Disney World parks, and on QVC. I pictured myself being interviewed on Good Morning America, sharing the story of my eating disorder and what it was like to start a business from my college dorm room at Georgetown University. I thought about what it would feel like to pitch on Shark Tank and have all the sharks advocating for why I should take their deal because they each are dying to get in on my quickly growing company.

This was the first day of the rest of my life—or at least I thought it was.

JANUARY 1, 2019

I opened the door to my grandmother's garage to see the hundreds of boxes of plates that no one wanted. Though a few boxes here and there were missing from the tall stacks, the boxes still took up the majority of the garage.

I placed my hand on the side of one of the boxes and wiped off the thick dust that had built up over the past year and a half. As I breathed in the dusty air, I felt a burning sensation in my throat. All of a sudden, my emotions hit me like a brick wall. I felt myself beginning to hyperventilate and, before I knew it, I found myself sitting on the garage floor in the same spot I sat the day those plates were delivered. This time, instead of dreaming about what was next, I broke out into uncontrollable tears. The pain I felt was massive and inescapable. It felt like I was just knocked over by a rough wave in the ocean, and now that I was underwater, more rough waves kept coming, preventing me from making my way up to the surface to breathe.

My plates were a total flop. The only people who actually bought them were my family and friends. You know, the people who love you so much they would literally buy anything you were selling? I could be selling poop, and my mom and her siblings would tell me it was the best poop they had ever seen.

Where was I going to go next? Should I just give up and get a job? Should I start a different business? I was confused and I felt like a total failure. I lost all belief in myself and my business.

As I gasped for air in between the heavy sobs, I knew something had to change. But my business didn't need to change—I did.

With red, swollen eyes and shaky legs, I grabbed onto the side of one of the boxes at the top of the stack and pulled my body back up. Though I was having trouble understanding why this was happening to me, something inside of me felt the need to thank the universe for this lesson.

Jim Carrey says, "Life doesn't happen to you. It happens for you."[1] I knew this incredibly challenging time was happening for a reason. I was ready to do the inner work and become the best version of myself so I could build the business I always dreamed of.

As T. Harv Eker, best-selling author of Secrets of the Millionaire Mind, says, "Your income can only grow to the extent you do."[2] Unsure where in the world I was headed next and $10,000 in debt, I took one final glance into the garage and, with a deep breath, I closed the door. It was time to embark on a new chapter of my life.

---

1   (Speakola, 2019)
2   (Eker, 2016)

YOUR FULL POTENTIAL

Most people never reach their full potential. They live a mediocre life, set mediocre goals, and convince themselves they're living the life they really want.

They say they don't want the responsibility of owning their own business or having millions of dollars in the bank.

The problem with this view is that it's completely self-sabotaging. Life is more fulfilling when you do work you love. I think everyone would agree with me on that one. And it's not too much of a stretch to say that most people would agree life would be easier if they had millions of dollars in the bank.

The real reason most people settle for mediocrity is fear. They are so deathly afraid to put themselves out there and take a risk. They don't want to feel the way I felt on January 1, 2019. But they fail to understand their success is inevitable, if only they would believe it was. And the truth is I would rather relive that day, when I cried my eyes out in my grandmother's garage, over and over again, than live a life wondering what if.

Looking back on my journey, I now know failure isn't only a part of the process, but it's actually the most important part of the process because it's where all the learning happens. And that learning is the secret sauce that brings you closer to achieving your goals. Because of this, I'm no longer afraid to put myself out there. If the worst thing that can possibly happen is actually a good thing that will help me get closer to achieving my goals, why the heck wouldn't I put myself out there?

I felt called to write this book because, for a long time, I found myself throwing spaghetti at the wall waiting for something to stick. The worst part was that it never did. I worked long hours every single day and had absolutely nothing to show for it. As a woman, I've personally faced the challenges most female entrepreneurs go through on their journeys to success. It took me three years to build a six-figure business, and my hope is by sharing the strategies that propelled me to success, I can help you achieve your goals even faster.

Even though women-owned businesses in the United States have grown by 114 percent in the past 20 years and currently account for 39 percent of all businesses, they still only account for 4.2 percent of total U.S business revenue.[3] This is incredibly alarming. It means millions of women are working their tails off without seeing the financial results they deserve. Money is a tool for impact, and the more we can get money in the hands of women, the more impact the world will see.

---

3   (Nawbo.org, 2019)

This book is not your typical business book. I believe hustle is not the answer. Instead, you must turn inward and start there. Much of what I am going to teach you is rooted in the power of mindset. The results you see in your life and business today are simply a mirror for what's going on in your mind. If you're not quite yet where you want to be, the answer is already inside of you to change your reality.

If you picked up this book because you're ready to live a life that is even better than anything you can possibly imagine, you're in the right place. My hope is it finds its way into the hands of female entrepreneurs like you, who are searching for actionable steps to grow their business and their mindset so they can step into the life and business of their dreams.

Some of my favorite stories you'll read in this book include:

- Why I stand in a power pose and talk to myself at 5 a.m. every morning and why you should too. (Chapter 2)
- The time I spent $15,000 on my business in a single day and why you should consider doing the same. (Chapter 6)
- How I manifested the exact car I was dreaming of and how you can manifest anything you desire. (Chapter 10)

If you're 100 percent committed to taking responsibility for your own life and doing the inner work to overcome the fears, limiting beliefs, and bad habits that have been holding you back, you're in the right place. I'm so thankful you have picked up this book and I know your life will be forever changed as a result of reading it. So, what are you waiting for? Let's get started.

PART 1:

CLARITY

CHAPTER 1:

STOP RUNNING IN CIRCLES

———

Imagine you are embarking on a cross country road trip with your best friend. The two of you have been looking forward to this trip for months. When you planned the trip, you weren't sure exactly where you wanted to go. All you knew was that you wanted to drive from the East Coast to the West Coast and you would figure out the rest along the way. Ever since you were little girls, the two of you have always talked about driving cross country together. Now it's finally happening!

Your car is filled to the brim with clothes, blankets, pillows, snacks, and drinks. You're planning on traveling for three months, so you've made sure to pack clothes for the various weather conditions in different geographies. Once all of your bags are in the car, it's time to say goodbye to loved ones. After saying your goodbyes, the two of you jump into your red Jeep and get ready to start driving.

Sipping on your hot Starbucks coffee, you begin to think about how you couldn't be more ready for this trip! As you get situated in the driver's seat, you realize you have one major problem: you haven't yet decided on a final destination. In fact, you haven't even decided where your first stop will be.

What should you type into your GPS?

Just like a driver without a destination, I see so many female entrepreneurs attempting to move closer to their goals without articulating what those goals actually are.

How can you expect step-by-step instructions on how to move from point A to point B without first knowing what point B is?

GETTING CLEAR ON YOUR BIG DREAMS

"Begin with the end in mind."

—STEVEN COVEY, AUTHOR OF THE 7 HABITS
OF HIGHLY EFFECTIVE PEOPLE[4]

As Steven Covey suggests, we're going to start by making clear on what "the end" looks like for you. Then, we're going to work backward to figure out where you should be headed today, so you will be one step closer to achieving your big dreams tomorrow.

Notice I said "big dreams," not "little dreams." It's time to stop playing small. Your dreams should be so big you feel embarrassed to say them out loud. Your dreams should scare you more than the most terrifying horror movie you've ever seen.

Your dreams should be so big you will still be working towards them at ninety years old.

I'm going to share with you some of my big dreams to inspire you to make your dreams as big as you can possibly imagine:

---

4   (Covey, 1999)

1. Build a billion dollar company.
2. Speak on stage at Rachel Hollis' RISE Business Conference.
3. Write a #1 New York Times best-selling book.
4. Donate millions of dollars to breast cancer research.

I have many more big dreams, but this book isn't about me. It's about you. So, it's time to start getting clear on what your big dreams are.

In order to do this, I want you to imagine a day in your dream life. Remember, in your dream life you can be, do, and have anything your heart desires. So, tell me, what does your life look like?

Notice I said your life, not your business. You have a choice to build your life around your business or your business around your life. Remember there are no rules. You can create anything you desire. I encourage you to first think about your dream life and then create a business that enables you to live that kind of life.

Below are a few questions to provoke thought if you're having a bit of trouble imagining your dream life.

Where do you live? Are you married? Do you have children? What time do you wake up in the morning? What does your morning routine consist of? What do you eat for breakfast? How many days per week do you exercise? What does your bedtime routine look like? Do you read often? What kind of car do you drive? Who do you spend the most time with? What do you do on the weekends? Do you travel often? If so, where to? Do you own a vacation home? If so, where? Do you donate money to nonprofits you are passionate about? If so, which nonprofits and how much money?

Spend some time meditating and journaling about your dream life. Don't put too much pressure on this. You don't have to have it all figured out today. All you need to do is start somewhere. You can always make changes to this vision of your dream life as your passions and desires change.

My big dreams went from pitching my plates on Shark Tank to coaching female entrepreneurs and helping them build their dream businesses. There was nothing wrong with me for making this shift. Most people put so much pressure on discovering your "purpose." I don't believe we are singular-purposed human beings.

We go through different seasons of life that may draw us to one passion for a while and another passion at another time. For example, when I was in the season of recovering from my eating disorder, I wanted to help other women who struggled with disordered eating. Then, when I was in the season of building my business, I wanted to help other women who were struggling with getting their companies off the ground. If we do have a "purpose," I believe it's much broader than we think. For example, my purpose is simply to help people. Through all the different seasons of my life, I've always found a way to go back to that purpose and help others.

I hope my journey gives you both clarity and confidence around the dreams you have today, knowing it's okay to change your mind as you grow through different stages of your life.

Now that you have a big picture, let's dive deeper into your business specifically. How much money does your business make? How much money do you pay yourself? Do you have your own office? If so, where? Do you have employees? If so, how many? Are they local or virtual? How many customers do you currently have? How does your business positively impact your customers? What kinds of testimonials and reviews have you received? How many hours a week do you work? What kind of work do you do on a daily basis? What are you most proud of? Have you received any recognitions or awards for your work?

If you don't yet have a clear picture of your big dreams, take a pause here. Remember to take the pressure off this exercise by giving yourself full freedom to update these dreams as you find more clarity. This step is important because it's absolutely critical that you have a clear picture of where you want to go before you move on to any of the additional exercises.

SETTING ONE-YEAR GOALS

Now that you have a clear picture of where you want to go, it's time to work backwards to create a plan for the next year in your business.

I wish I could tell you there was an exact science to this. Something like: take your dream and divide it by fifty, and the result is where you should be one year from today. But in reality, plans don't work like this.

As Henry Ford says, "Whether you think you can, or you think you can't—you're right."[5]

Your success is a product of what you believe is possible for you.

I've personally experienced falling short on goals simply because I didn't believe they were possible for me more times than I'd like to admit. When I first started my business (like most newbie entrepreneurs) I had very little patience.

---

5   (Goodreads.com, 2019)

I set HUGE, unrealistic goals for myself. In two months, I planned on growing my Instagram account by 500,000 followers. (Note: It's important for me to mention I actually don't believe this goal is "unrealistic." Reality is simply a reflection of what's going on in our minds, so you can achieve anything you believe you can. The reason it was unrealistic for me was because I didn't actually believe I could achieve this goal.)

After a week or two of working toward my lofty goal, I felt discouraged. A few days later, I gave up on my goal. Here's the thing. If you set a goal you don't feel confident in, you will eventually feel discouraged and give up.

Because of this, I recommend you set your one-year goal by asking yourself, "What is the biggest goal I can possibly imagine that I feel 100 percent confident I can achieve?"

Remember this is a rule only for goals. Your dreams should be so big that maybe you don't even believe they are possible (yet). Understand that dreams are the culmination of achieving all of your goals throughout your life. Goals are the small steps that bring you closer to your dreams. Goals have deadlines. Dreams do not.

As you set your one-year goal, push your limits as much as you can while still holding onto the belief that it is possible for you. Step just outside our comfort zone in this goal. Go one level beyond what you think you can.

By this point, you should have an idea of what your one year goal will be.

Got it? Good because this is where the magic happens.

Dr. Gail Matthews, a psychology professor at the Dominican University of California, found you are 42 percent more likely to achieve your goals if you write them down.[6]

We're going to take this a step further. Did you know your brain doesn't know the difference between real and imagined? Remember that cross country road trip? Your brain doesn't know if it actually happened or if it was simply something you thought about.

In 1995, the National Institute of Health conducted a study where volunteers were asked to play a sequence of piano notes for five consecutive days.[7] Another set of volunteers was asked, instead, to simply imagine playing the sequence of notes. Brain scans were conducted daily on each participant in the two groups.

---

6   (Inc.com, 2019)
7   (David R Hamilton PhD, 2019)

The changes in the brain of those who imagined playing the piano were the same as those who actually played the piano. Why is this important and how does this relate to your goals?

If your brain doesn't understand the difference between real and imagined, and you write your goals as if you have already achieved them, the changes in your brain will be based on the belief you actually *have* achieved them. This will lead to greater confidence, which, in turn, will help you *actually* achieve the goal.

Because of this powerful science, you should write your goal in the following format: "It is now (insert date one year from today) and I have (insert goal in past tense)."

For example, it is now January 1, 2021, and I have generated $100,000 in revenue in my business in the past year.

Or, it is now January 1, 2021, and I am the proud author of a bestselling book.

If you want to add even more power to this goal, write it somewhere you will see it on a daily basis. One of my favorite spots is on a Post-it note or on your mirror. A whiteboard in your office or on your refrigerator are also great places to display your goal. The more you see this goal, the more those feelings will be reinforced that it has already happened.

SETTING YOUR NINETY-DAY GOAL

In order to make you one-year goal a reality, we need to break it down even further. This is the most challenging step for most of my clients because I only allow them to pick one goal to focus on for the next ninety days.

In his bestselling book *The ONE Thing*, Gary Keller challenges readers to ask the powerful question, "What is the ONE Thing I can do such that by doing it, everything else will be easier or unnecessary?"[8]

In order to achieve a goal, you need to go all in on that one goal.

Imagine you are standing in a garden. In this garden there are many beautiful flowers. Each of these flowers represents a goal you have. Unfortunately, we are in a terrible drought and you only are allotted one cup of water per day to water your flowers. You have two choices: a) sprinkle the water across the whole garden so each flower gets a little water or b) pour the whole cup of water on a single flower.

---

8   (Keller and Papasan, 2013)

If you choose choice A, you will end up with a dead garden. A sprinkle of water is not enough to sustain any of the flowers. However, if you choose choice B, you will have a beautiful flower that has bloomed.

That water is representative of your time, energy, and money— all things that are limited.

So tell me, what is the one thing you will focus on over the next ninety days? Which flower matters more than any of the other plants in your garden? Which of your goals makes you feel most excited to jump out of bed in the morning? Which of your goals are you most excited to tell your best friend about?

Again, you'll want to write your goal as if it has already happened. "It is now (insert date ninety days from today) and I have (insert goal in past tense)."

Now that you have broken down your big dreams into one small focused goal, it's time to get out there and make it your reality!

HOW TO APPLY THIS CHAPTER TO YOUR LIFE TODAY:

1. Write down five big dreams you have for your life.
2. Write down five big dreams you have for your business.
3. Write down your one-year and ninety-day goals in the past tense.
4. Post these goals on your mirror, refrigerator, whiteboard, or somewhere else you will see them daily.

CHAPTER 2:

STOP UNDERESTIMATING THE POWER OF YOUR MIND

———

In 1985, a nineteen-year-old boy named Jim headed to Hollywood to pursue his dreams of being an actor and comedian. Broke and depressed, Jim drove around his beat-up Toyota, daydreaming about success. Four years earlier, Jim performed his first comedy show in Toronto and was booed off the stage. He had a long way to go, but he was determined to achieve his dreams.

As you know, working towards a big dream can, at times, be pretty discouraging. One cool November day, in an attempt to raise his spirits, Jim decided to write himself check for $10 million, dated ten years in the future for "acting services rendered." Through ups and downs, Jim carried this check with him everywhere he went.

After a few years of wear and tear in his wallet, the check slowly began to deteriorate. Regardless of the check's declining appearance, Jim continued to carry it around with him, knowing someday his daydream would be real. No matter how many times he failed, no matter how many people told him no, Jim knew deep down his success was inevitable and someday this check would be real.

It's no coincidence that exactly ten years later, just before Thanksgiving 1995, Jim Carrey found out he was cast in the movie *Dumb and Dumber* for $10 million.[9]

THE POWER OF VISUALIZATION

"Your outer world is a reflection of your inner world."

—T. HARV EKER[10]

According to the Law of Attraction, you attract what you focus on. The reality you see and live every day is simply a mirror for what is going on in your mind.

---

9   (Hoffman, 2019)
10   (Eker, 2016)

Dr. Judd Biasiotto at the University of Chicago decided to do some research on this theory. He split volunteers into three groups and tested how many free throws they could make. Then, he required group one to practice free throws every day for an hour, group two to visualize themselves making free throws, and group three to do nothing.

Group one improved by 24 percent from practicing free throws every day. But get this: group two, who only visualized themselves making free throws, improved by 23 percent.[11] How mind blowing is that?

This is why so many people attribute their success not to talent or hard work, but to visualization. Olympic swimmer Michael Phelps visualized every single detail of the moment he would win an Olympic gold medal. He committed to this practice twice a day, every day. It's no wonder that today he has racked up a total of twenty-three Olympic gold medals.[12]

If you want to attract more success into your life, you must commit to a daily practice of visualization. An easy way to do this is to picture your "champagne moment." Imagine you are sharing a bottle of champagne with the people who matter most to you, in celebration of your success. You have

---

11   (Haefner, 2019)
12   (Sparks, 2019)

just accomplished the biggest goals you can possibly imagine for your life and your business.

Picture this scene in vivid detail. Where are you? Who are you with? What are you wearing? What are the people you are with wearing? How do you feel? What does the champagne taste like? Is there food at this celebration? If so, what kind of food is it? What does it smell like? What does it taste like? For maximum effectiveness, imagine being inside of yourself, looking at the scene from your own eyes.

I recommend you commit to a specific time of day where you will visualize your champagne moment every single day.

Another way to practice visualization is to actually act as if you already have the success you desire in real life. For example, do your dreams involve buying a certain type of car? Let's say you dream of driving a Porsche. What color is your dream Porsche? Are the seats leather? What special features does it have? Go to your local dealer and test drive that exact model today. See what it feels like to sit inside of it, to drive it, and simply for it to be yours. Pretend it is, and soon enough it will be. I also highly recommend you document this moment. Take a photo or video of you inside your dream car. It will be amazing for you to be able to look back one day to see where you started and where you are now.

Maybe one of your big dreams is buying a beachfront home. Start attending open houses as if you already have the money you desire to purchase this home, and it won't be long until you do. When you're at an open house, ask yourself the following questions. What do you love about this home? What would you change? If you were going to purchase this home, what color would you paint the kitchen? What about your bedroom? What decor and furniture would match the aesthetic of this home?

The more detail you imagine, the more real this will feel. The more real it feels, the more likely you are to make this dream your reality.

As you may remember, one of my big dreams is to donate millions of dollars to breast cancer research. I've already written out a check for $5 million, dated ten years in the future, addressed to the "Breast Cancer Research Foundation," whose mission is "to prevent and cure breast cancer by advancing the world's most promising research." If there is an organization you are passionate about, I suggest you follow in my footsteps (or really Jim Carrey's footsteps) and write out your donation, too.

Keep in mind that the bigger your financial goals are, the more impact you can have on the world. Money is simply a tool for impact. A visualization for a charitable donation is especially good for you if you struggle with any limiting beliefs around the idea that rich people are greedy. You will learn more about this in chapter four, so keep this visualization practice in mind when you do.

AFFIRMATIONS

On average, we have about 60,000 to 80,000 thoughts per day.[13] The scary part is that 95 percent of them are the same thoughts we had yesterday and the day before that. And here's what's even scarier, we don't even realize we are having majority of our thoughts because they occur on a subconscious level.

Your thoughts are the result of deeply ingrained beliefs that live in your subconscious mind, which was programmed in your first seven years of life. Think about all the things you were told about who you are supposed to be when you were a child.

"Oh, she's just a little shy."

"She's going to be a doctor when she grows up."

"She's always wanted to follow in her father's footsteps and become a lawyer."

---

13 (Sasson, 2019)

"You must finish all the food on your plate or you won't grow tall and strong."

"You're just not a math person."

These beliefs about who you were supposed to be formed your identity. Your actions are deeply impacted by who you are on an identity level. If you believe you're "shy," you will likely never volunteer to speak in front of a large group of people, even though in reality you are just as capable as anyone else. If you believe you're "not a math person," you will likely ignore all the numbers in your business, even though the big picture requires very little math, if any.

Although your parents, teachers, and other significant figures in your childhood had positive intentions, these repeated phrases formed into subconscious beliefs that hold you back from being who you truly are and unlocking your maximum potential for success.

Much of our life's successes and failures are a direct result of the beliefs in our subconscious mind.

Therefore, if you're not happy with the success you currently have in your life, you must reprogram your subconscious beliefs. Only then will you step into the success you've always wanted.

One way to reprogram your subconscious mind is to repeat affirmations to yourself over and over again, until your subconscious mind accepts the affirmation as truth and forms a new belief.

Every morning, before I start my day, I stand in a power pose (with my hands on my hips) and I choose three affirmations to repeat over and over again out loud. When I first started this practice, my mom thought I was crazy because she would hear me talking to myself at 5 a.m. Now that she often travels across the country with me to speaking engagements, she knows my crazy 5 a.m. talk actually works. In fact, she picked up this "crazy" practice herself!

I learned one of my favorite affirmations from Kathrin Zenkina, founder of Manifestation Babe. Kathrin says, "My success is inevitable, and I am always on the right path." This affirmation is fantastic for female entrepreneurs because it reminds you, even when you're feeling down, you are exactly where you need to be and nothing is stopping you from achieving the success you desire.

You can repeat affirmations anytime. Though repeating them in your head is better than not at all, I find it makes a big difference when I say mine out loud. I often find myself repeating affirmations while I'm driving alone or taking a shower. On days where I'm lacking confidence, I repeat my affirmations throughout the day to reinforce beliefs I would like to instill in my mind.

Other affirmations I often say are:

- Money flows to me easily, effortlessly, and abundantly.
- I am open and ready to attract anything I desire.
- Each day I am making my dreams a reality.
- I always have more than enough money to pay my bills and expenses.
- My biggest breakthrough is around the corner.
- My potential is limitless.
- I can do anything I put my mind to.
- I am a money magnet.
- I am a client magnet.

Feel free to come up with your own affirmations that resonate with you. This is especially important in areas of your life where limiting beliefs may be holding you back. Now is a good time to ask yourself if there are any specific beliefs you may be holding onto that have been holding you back? If any come up, be sure to come up with an affirmation you can repeat to help you overcome the limiting belief.

BE DO HAVE MODEL

Most people assume that first you will *have* the thing you desire, say a million dollar business. Then, because you have a million dollar business, you will *do* the things you need to do to run the million dollar business, and finally you will *be* the million dollar CEO.

In reality, quite the opposite is true. First, you need to *be* the person who *does* the things a million dollar CEO would do. Only after you be and do will you actually *have* the million dollar business. This is often known as "acting as if."

When you break this model down, it seems like common sense. You don't first have a medal from running a marathon, then run the training runs, and finally become a runner. Instead, you first become a runner, then you commit to doing the things runners do, like training runs, and finally you will have the medal from completing your first marathon.

Yet if this is such common sense, why do most people fail to dedicate time each day into "being" the person they need to be and doing the things they need to do in order to achieve their goals?

To simplify this model, write a list of who you will be when you achieve your biggest dreams. For inspiration, here is my list:

- A leader
- Committed
- Happy
- Successful
- Inspirational
- Innovative
- Proud
- Generous
- Secure
- Confident

The first step to implementing this model is recognizing you already are all of the things on your list because each of the characteristics is within you. For example, I am already a leader because I lead my team, my students, and my followers. I am already happy because I am building the career of my dreams and I have the best support system.

But Jaclyn, what about things I really feel like I'm not? For example, what if you wrote "wealthy" on your list and, currently, you struggle to pay your bills each month? First, recognize any ways that, regardless of your bank account balance, you are already wealthy. Maybe you have great health or amazing friends. Remember there are other ways to measure wealth.

Second, focus on acting as if you are wealthy (or whatever you feel like you're not). To step into this, ask yourself

"What would the CEO of a million dollar company do in this situation?"

This doesn't mean you should go buy yourself a private jet when you can barely afford your monthly credit card bill. Remember that wealthy people respect their money, and to act wealthy, you need to respect yours too. Rather, it means to make decisions from a place of success. The million dollar CEO would hire a virtual assistant for three dollars an hour from the Philippines to take additional tasks off their plate.

Finally, dedicate time on a daily basis to becoming this person. If you don't feel like you're a good leader, what books can your read or what podcasts can you listen to that will help you become a better leader. If you aren't generous, what organizations can you donate to today? Remember, this doesn't have to be a lot of money. Maybe you can give a ten-dollar donation to a cause you are passionate about. By investing your time and energy into becoming the person you need to be, you will soon be doing the things you need to do and, before you know it, you will have achieved all of the dreams that currently feel out of reach.

HOW TO APPLY THIS CHAPTER TO YOUR LIFE TODAY:

1. Commit to either a morning or bedtime daily visualization practice (or both).

2. Pick at least one affirmation that resonates with you and repeat it to yourself out loud while you are in the shower or while you are driving.

3. Write a list of who you will be when you achieve your goals and begin to act as that person today.

CHAPTER 3:

STOP SPEAKING SO NEGATIVELY

———

A few months ago, I decided to run a little experiment with my thoughts. At the time, I was working toward a goal of my first $20,000 month in my business.

To aid in my efforts, I made a commitment to only speak in a way that brought me closer to my goal. Every time I felt like I was going to fall short, I found a way to reframe the situation. "Maybe this wasn't my big break, but I know it's is coming very soon."

At first, this felt like quite a silly experiment. I was saying those words, but deep down I didn't actually believe they were true. I often felt discouraged and wanted to give up on my goal.

Even at my lowest moments, I committed to finding a positive way to frame each situation. I figured if it didn't help me reach my goal that month, I would write it off as a waste of time. But it was worth at least giving it my all for one month.

Then, about three weeks in, something magical happened. Something in my brain clicked, and I finally started to believe the words I was saying. And, because I finally believed my words, my actions started changing. I put myself out there and showed up more than I ever had before.

I remember one day toward the end of the month, I felt particularly down. I had not been making as much progress toward my goal as I would have liked. In the past, whenever I felt discouraged, I usually either gave up on my goal or shrink my goal to something I knew I could achieve. This time, instead of saying something like "There's no way I'm going to hit my goal," instead I said "I haven't quite gotten there yet but soon I will be."

With that internal confidence shift, instead of retreating in my efforts, I wholeheartedly committed to doing whatever it took to achieve my goal. My mind began to dream about possibilities. Who can I talk to that might be able to introduce me to a potential client? Who should I reach out to who could benefit from my coaching programs? What about the tall blonde woman I met at that networking event a few weeks back? As hard as I tried, I couldn't turn my mind off even when I wanted to.

I remember one day I was in the middle of a manicure, thinking: I need to open notes on my phone and write down all of these ideas! When I woke up the next morning, I got to work on all of my big plans. I began connecting with new people and confidently putting the offer for my program out there into the world.

On the last day of the month, I closed the final sale that brought me over the $20,000 mark. In fact, I actually surpassed my goal, bringing in over $23,000. I couldn't believe the direct impact changing my language had on my success, but I knew I was onto a secret that most people go their whole life without discovering.

WHAT REALLY HAPPENED

At the time, I didn't quite understand that changing my words wasn't the game changer. It was the fact that, by changing my words, I actually changed my thoughts.

Mildred Lisette Norman, the "Peace Pilgrim," said, "If you realized how powerful your thoughts are, you would never think a negative thought."[14]

We all have heard it before: your thoughts become your words, your words become your actions, and your actions become the results you see in your life. Therefore, if you're not happy with your life, you have to change your thoughts.

While I had read about this concept in many books, it always seemed so difficult for me to actually change my thoughts. After all, we aren't even consciously aware of 95 percent of our thoughts. For years I attempted to "think positively," but most of the time it was just an external mask I put on to hide the negative way I was feeling inside.

It wasn't until I did this little experiment that I realized the easiest way to change your thoughts is to first change your words. In the words of Robert Kiyosaki, bestselling author of Rich Dad Poor Dad, "If you want to change your life, begin by changing your words. Start speaking the words of your dreams, of who you want to become, not the words of fear or failure."[15]

---

14 (Ranker, 2019)
15 (Motivation, 2019)

Changing your words builds your belief that you are capable of achieving even your biggest dreams. When I was a kid, my dad used to tell me, "You can do anything you put your mind to," just about every single day. This positive reinforcement built my self-belief that I really was capable of anything I wanted to achieve. Over the years, especially after many failures in entrepreneurship, I lost sight of this belief.

By changing my language, as well as practicing affirmations, visualization, and other concepts taught in this book, I rebuilt my confidence in my own ability to make it happen. As my first business coach Terri Levine says, "Find a way or make a way." I know I am in control of my own destiny, therefore I will always find a way to make it work.

The other special thing that happens when you speak the words of your dreams is you meet people who can help you. Just yesterday, I gave a speech where I mentioned my big dream of speaking on Rachel Hollis' stage. A few minutes after the speech, one of the audience members approached me and explained that he knows Rachel Hollis and would love to connect us. He couldn't make any promises but offered to see where it would take me.

Ladies, if I didn't put my big dream out there, no one would have read my mind and thought, "Maybe I should introduce this girl to Rachel Hollis." So, it's time to speaking the words of your dreams because you never know who is listening! If you're a Rachel Hollis fan, maybe you'll be seeing me speak at the next Rise Business Conference—remember you never know unless you try!

THE "NO" LIST

After the life-changing results of my little experiment, I decided to create a "no" list filled with words that are off-limits in my vocabulary. Below, I've shared my "no" list with you in hopes that it becomes your "no" list too. I've also shared the reframes I use to make it as easy as possible for you to start implementing these language shifts today.

Making a commitment to remove these words and phrases from my vocabulary has truly skyrocketed my success. Don't believe me? Simply try it for one month and let your results speak for themselves.

My "No" List:

- Struggling (Instead of "I'm struggling" you can say, "This isn't quite right yet." Yet implies that it will be right soon.)
- Expensive (Expensive is in direct relation to how much money you have. Warren Buffet probably wouldn't think a fifty-dollar steak dinner is expensive. Instead, talk

about the value of something, which is only in direct relation to what the item is worth, not how much money you have. Replace expensive with words like "overpriced" or "overvalued.")

- Hard (Instead of "This is so hard," ask yourself how you can make what you are working on easy and enjoyable. If you don't feel there is a way to make the task "easy and enjoyable," instead say, "This is a necessary part of the process and I am thankful for its teachings." Here, you are acknowledging the positives even in times that aren't as sunny.)

- Overwhelmed/Stressed/Busy (Instead of complaining about being "overwhelmed" or "stressed," you can say something like "I'm grateful for the abundant opportunities filling my schedule right now." I also included busy in this section because we need to stop bragging about how busy we are and instead focus on spending time more intentionally.)

- Can't Afford (Instead of complaining that you "can't afford" a manicure, focus on how "getting a manicure is so luxurious.")

- Confused / Lost (You're not "confused" or "lost," you are simply "in the process of finding clarity.")

- Stuck (Instead, say "my breakthrough is around the corner.")

- Tired (Instead, say "I had a productive day, and I will now give my body the time it needs to rest.")

If, after implementing the "no" list, it has made a positive impact on your life, please share it with any loved ones who you think would be open to these mindset shifts. The more people who speak positively, the more light and joy we can spread to the world! Together, we can set the world on fire!

REFRAMING STRATEGIES

As you can see from my reframing suggestions, changing your language isn't about painting everything as sunshine and rainbows, though many people jump to conclusions that it is.

In fact, some of my biggest business breakthroughs came when I learned to embrace and appreciate chaos. I used to think, at some point, you would hit a place in your business where everything was peaceful and there were only ups.

I quickly learned it's actually in the downs where you learn the most valuable lessons. And without those lessons, you will never have the ups. This is why it's important to acknowledge where you are while appreciating where you are going. And where you are going is always better than where you are.

As a part of my daily gratitude practice, I often look for the "downs." When I receive a large bill in the mail, like my mortgage, I feel incredibly blessed that I own a home. I'm thankful for my cell phone bill because it allows me to communicate with loved ones and run my business. I'm thankful for my cable bill because it brings me down time and relaxation. I'm thankful for my gym membership because it means I have a body that is physically able to exercise. I pay each and every bill with immense gratitude for the luxurious in my life. Finding gratitude in things most people complain about is a great way to focus on using our language to move us forward, not hold us back.

The biggest breakthrough I had with "positive thinking" was realizing it's not about pretending things are wonderful when they're not. It's about shifting your perspective to see the positives in any situation. It's about putting your focus not on where you are today, but on where you want to go tomorrow.

As you begin to implement the "no" list into your daily routine, you will be shocked at how often you find yourself saying these negative, self-sabotaging words and phrases. When I first started abiding by the "no" list, I constantly found myself saying off-limit words without even realizing I was thinking them.

The easiest way to correct this is simply to reword your sentence after it comes out of your mouth. For example, imagine you're talking to a friend and you happen to say, "Those shoes are so expensive." As soon as you recognize you said one of the words on the "no" list, simply say, "What I meant to say is those shoes are overpriced. I respect my money and don't see the value in spending $200 on a pair of sandals."

If the person you are speaking to has a growth mindset, tell him or her about the "no" list and why you are making a conscious effort to change your language. On the other hand, if the person you are speaking to would roll their eyes at this concept, don't worry about explaining yourself. Chances are they won't even notice you reworded your sentence. I've been doing this for months and have never once been questioned. Most people are too concerned with what's going to come out of their own mouths next to question what's just come out of yours.

One last tip I have that has been instrumental in helping me shift my language is to film a video of yourself on your phone talking about the way you feel when you are tempted to use words on the "no" list. Allow yourself to speak freely and use whatever words come to mind. I often do this when I am working through a decision in my life or my business.

Once you've filmed the video, watch it back and write down all of the "no" list words or phrases you used. Then, film a new video of yourself using reframes for each of those words. You will be impressed by how easy it is to change your language once you've identified the words and phrases that are holding you back.

HOW TO APPLY THIS CHAPTER TO YOUR LIFE TODAY:

1. Commit to eliminating using words and phrases on the "no" list from your vocabulary for a minimum of thirty days.

2. Reword sentences after you've accidentally said words on the "no" list.

3. If you have a decision to make and are tempted to use words on the "no" list, film a video of yourself talking out your feelings, write down all self-sabotaging words used, and re-film the video using more positive language.

CHAPTER 4:

STOP SAYING MONEY DOESN'T GROW ON TREES

——

When I was a kid, I didn't really understand the concept of money or how much we had. Sometimes I would dream up grandiose ideas that were clearly not in our budget. Like the time I wanted my dad to build a stable in our small suburban backyard and buy me a pony. That's when he would respond, "You know Jaclyn, money doesn't grow on trees." As you now know, this seemingly innocent phrase my parents told me over and over again actually formed a subconscious belief that impacted my thoughts, feelings, and actions throughout the years.

Now, we all know money doesn't actually grow on trees. Unless you like to be devil's advocate, in which case, money is paper, and paper comes from trees. Jokes aside, this expression that money doesn't grow on trees translates to the belief that in order to make money, you must work hard.

Now, I'm not about to discredit hard work. In fact, I'm a huge advocate for taking action and committing to your goals.

The problem with this belief lies in the assumption that, in order to make more money, you have to work harder. When does more end? Can you "hustle" your way to a million dollar company? What about a billion dollar company? If the only way you can make money is to work hard, that would mean you could never make passive income. It is often said that the average millionaire has seven streams of income. Do you think every millionaire is "hustling" to make money in each of those seven streams?

This belief held me back for a long time. I often worked eighty-hour weeks (more on this in chapter 8) and had little to show for it the majority of the time. If money really did come from hard work, I should have been rich already with all the hard work I was putting in.

It wasn't until I replaced this belief with a new belief that focused on how easy it was for me to make money that unexpected sources of money came into my life.

I'm not talking about pennies on the ground (though who doesn't love a good lucky penny). I'm talking about large amounts of money. What's really cool about this as a business owner is that I assumed the only money I could manifest would be through sales in my business. This was far from true. I've manifested thousands of dollars in my personal life as well as odd ways that had nothing to do with my core business itself. If this sparks your interest, keep reading. I dive deep into the manifestation process in chapter 10!

Like when my fiancé and I found out we owed $25,000 less than we had originally budgeted for in closing costs on the purchase of our home. Or when I was given the gift of free office space in exchange for mentoring a local entrepreneur. Or when I got paid two weeks early for an upcoming speech.

Ladies, all of these things happened within just a couple months of each other. Not so ironically, it was right after I did the work to change my money mindset. This is all possible for you too. The first step to changing your beliefs is identifying what your beliefs actually are.

COMMON MONEY BELIEFS

Just like my parents often told me "money doesn't grow on trees," there were probably sayings about money that you often heard as a child. Maybe your parents or teachers said things like:

- "More money, more problems"
- "Rich people are greedy"
- "Money is the root of all evil"
- "The rich get richer and the poor get poorer"
- "Money is a limited resource"
- "Another day, another dollar"
- "A penny saved is a penny earned"
- "Money doesn't buy happiness"

How many times have you heard these sayings in your life? It's no wonder so many people struggle with their money mindset! Remember that most of your subconscious beliefs form from birth to seven years old. Think back on your childhood and, specifically, any experiences related to money that you remember. How have those experiences created beliefs about money that you may still be holding onto?

Grab a pen and paper and write down any significant experiences relating to money from your childhood that you can remember, as well as any sayings about money you often heard. Next, write down what the belief behind that experience or saying is.

For example, if your parents were constantly struggling to pay the bills, you may have a belief that "there is never enough money." Or, if your parents often argued over money, you may think "money causes relationship problems."

To make this easier for you, I've listed out the belief associated with each of the common phrases about money I referenced above. Some are self-explanatory, while others need a bit more digging to uncover the belief.

- The saying "More money, more problems" correlates to the belief that money causes problems.
- The saying "Rich people are greedy" correlates to the belief that rich people only care about themselves.
- The saying "Money is the root of all evil" correlates to the belief that accumulating wealth makes you a bad person.
- The saying "The rich get richer and the poor get poorer" correlates to the belief that rich people do not help poor people.
- The saying "Money is a limited resource" correlates to the belief that there is never enough money for everyone.

- The saying "Another day, another dollar" correlates to the belief that you have to work hard every day to make money.
- The saying "A penny saved is a penny earned" correlates to the belief that you should always save your money instead of spending it.
- The saying "Money doesn't buy happiness" correlates to the belief that poor people and rich people have the same opportunities to be happy.

The combination of each of your money beliefs is your money story.

One common phrase used to describe a negative money story, coined by Stephen Covey in *The 7 Habits of Highly Effective People*, is scarcity mindset because it's rooted in the belief that money is a scarce resource.[16] The opposite of a scarcity mindset is an abundance mindset because it's rooted in the belief that there is plenty of money to go around.

If you make only one shift in your money mindset, I recommend you adapt an abundant mindset. Here are a few examples of the way a person with a scarcity mindset thinks versus the way a person with an abundant mindset thinks.

---

16   (Covey, 1999)

SCARCITY MINDSET

Feels anxious when they spend money. Often will physically resist spending when possible.

Focuses on the things they don't have.

Feels like there is never enough money.

Keeps all of their money for themself.

Sees obstacles.

Thinks small.

Focuses on what's not working.

ABUNDANCE MINDSET

Knows that for every dollar they spend, even more will come back to them.

Focuses on the things they do have.

Believes there is always more where that came from.

Is generous and often donates their money.

Sees opportunities.

Thinks big.

Focuses on what is working.

CHANGING YOUR MONEY STORY

Now that you've identified what your money story is, it's time to change it so you can step into the limitless potential inside of you. If you're not actively doing the work to change your money story, you are actively getting in your own way.

For each belief you've identified, ask yourself if there has ever been a time in your life where this belief wasn't true. For example, if one of your beliefs is "Rich people only care about themselves," ask yourself if you have ever met a rich person who cared about other people. Most likely, your answer will be yes. In fact, I personally know many more generous rich people than selfish rich people.

Or, if one of your beliefs is "Money causes problems," ask yourself if you know any wealthy people who have less problems than you? Maybe their lives are easier because they don't have to cut coupons or shop for deals. Instead, they can spend money on things that save them their precious time so they can spend more of it with loved ones.

If you don't personally know someone, take a look at the statistics. The number one reason for divorce in the United States is disagreements over money. If you had millions of dollars, you would likely argue less with your significant other and thus have less problems.

Starting to get the hang of this? If you really want to do the work, I recommend you write down at least one example that proves each belief isn't always true. The final step is to write a new belief you want to embrace.

Again, to make this easier for you to implement, below I've listed a suggestion for a new belief for each limiting belief.

- The belief that money causes problems can be replaced with the belief that money is simply a tool and makes it easier to solve problems when they inevitably arise, regardless of your financial position.
- The beliefs that rich people only care about themselves, accumulating wealth makes you a bad person, and rich people do not help poor people can be replaced with a belief that the more money you make, the more money you give to others.
- The belief that there is never enough money for everyone can be replaced with a belief that there is more than enough money for everyone in the abundant world we live in.

- The belief that you have to work hard every day to make money can be replaced with the belief that money flows to you easily, effortlessly, and abundantly.
- The belief that you should always save your money instead of spending it can be replaced with the belief that it is healthy to spend money on things that make you feel abundant.
- The belief that poor people and rich people have the same opportunities to be happy can be replaced with the belief that money is a tool for freedom, and the more freedom you have, the easier it is for you to be happy. Keep in mind this one is tricky because if you think money will actually buy you happiness, you probably have a scarcity mindset, and will be disappointed when it doesn't. If you focus on the abundance mindset, you will be happy with what you have now, so you can continue to be happy with what you have as you become wealthier and you have even more freedom.

You won't adapt a new money story overnight, but the more you say and write your new beliefs, the more you will begin to believe them, and eventually, you will align your actions with these new beliefs. This is why implementing the new beliefs you feel are holding you back the most into your daily affirmation routine is critical.

WHY THIS MATTERS

You may be wondering why I am suggesting you spend time working on your money mindset when you have a million other things you should be working on in your business.

At the end of the day, a business' goal is to make money. While impact is important, and more income drives more impact, if your end goal was impact, you would be a non-profit, not a business.

A note on this: I find so many women who feel greedy setting big financial goals for their business. When I tell them I'm on the road to a multi-million dollar company, they immediately become uncomfortable. This can be traced back to limiting money beliefs, specifically the ones related to rich people hoarding all their money and being evil people.

In reality, money is a tool for impact. If you want to change the world, it's going to be much easier to do it with a few million dollars (or better yet, a few billion dollars) than simply with your time. If your business is impact-driven, meaning the product or service you offer helps people, the more money your business makes, the more people you have helped. Then, with the profits you pay yourself, you can use that money to do good in the world in any areas you are passionate about. It's a total win-win.

Therefore, if your goal is to make money, the maximum amount of money you can make is determined by the size of your money mindset.

I want you to think of your money mindset like a container. Most people start with a super tiny container, like the kind you put salad dressing in when you pack a lunch.

How much money can you physically fit into that tiny dressing container? Not much before it begins to spill out the sides and shutting the lid becomes impossible. What if you decide to change the size of your container? Now, instead of a dressing container, you have a big lasagna tray, the kind that takes up your whole oven.

Now your container can hold a lot of money. It would take quite a while to fill it up. Eventually, you'll fill up this container, too, and you'll be challenged once again to go bigger.

The inner work never ends. It's a constant battle to become an even better version of yourself than you were yesterday. The good news is that the more energy you give your mindset, the more you will see it physically manifest into your bank account. I challenge you to commit to doing the work each and every day to level up your money mindset so you can create both the income and impact you desire.

HOW TO APPLY THIS CHAPTER TO YOUR LIFE TODAY:

1. Make a list of all of your beliefs about money.
2. Find at least one example of how each limiting belief isn't always true.
3. Make a list of the new beliefs that you will implement.

CHAPTER 5:

STOP SETTING A TIMELINE ON YOUR DREAMS

———

"I'm going to give up on my business and get a regular job," I casually told my dad as we were eating dinner one night, about two years into my entrepreneurial journey.

"You're what?" My dad was so surprised he started choking on the water he had just sipped. He couldn't believe what he just heard. Then I saw the disappointment begin to sink in. He looked at me and uttered, "Jaclyn, you are not a quitter." He politely put his fork down and walked out of the kitchen, leaving a half-eaten plate of chicken, veggies, and rice. As he left the room, I heard his words echo in my head over and over again. I began to think deeply about who I was, what I really wanted for my life, and how I was going to turn this around.

**

Needless to say, I decided to continue pursuing my dreams, even when I felt like they were taking far too long.

Just one year later, I've spoken at more than seventy-five colleges and conferences across the country and I've personally coached dozens of women, helping them make their dream business a reality. One of my clients recently told me I was the first person in her life to ever tell her that her biggest dreams were indeed possible.

What would have happened if I had given up on that day I felt discouraged? How many women would dim their light and sell themselves short because they never met someone who saw the potential inside of them?

If you have a dream in your heart, that dream is there for a reason. It was divinely placed inside of you by the universe, by God, by your higher power, so you could actualize it into your reality. The universe doesn't make any mistakes. That dream is there because you are supposed to pursue it.

This doesn't mean you will achieve your goals overnight, but it does mean they are worth it.

THE POWER OF PERSISTENCE

"A river cuts through rock not because of its power, but because of its persistence."

—JIM WATKINS.[17]

Girl, I get it. When you first start your business, you are so ready for your success that you want it to happen overnight. Please know you are not alone. I was the same way when I first started my business. In fact, most female entrepreneurs are.

My fiancé Richie always jokes around that when they interview him about my success (because that's going to happen, ladies) on Good Morning America someday, he's going to tell the story of when I was absolutely devastated because one factory told me they couldn't make my plates. He loves this story because it shows how far I've come.

When he says I was devastated, it's no exaggeration. I was lying-in-bed-for-days-could-barely-get-myself-to-class dev-

---

17 (passiton.com, 2019)

astated. Richie ended up sending me flowers to cheer me up, in hopes I would realize that someone telling me no was not the end of the world. Eventually, as time went on, I started to develop my persistence muscle and I learned that no simply means this is not the right person or the right time for a yes, but it doesn't mean I won't get the yes. It just means I need to find another way. When something doesn't go the way I wanted it to in my business, I immediately ask myself, how can I make this work? Is there an easier way? What path haven't I thought about yet?

The truth is, as Gary Vaynerchuk says, "Everything takes longer thank you think."[18] The entrepreneurs who "make it" are the ones who fully believe their success is inevitable and, therefore, always find a way to make it work.

They persevere even when they don't know where to turn. They accept full responsibility for the success of their business and they commit to the ups and downs of the journey.

I believe success is a choice. You get to decide each and every day if you want to continue working towards your dreams or let them die inside of you. It doesn't matter how many times you fall flat on your face. What matters is that you continue to stand back up, every single time.

---

18   (Improve Conversation, 2019)

Robert Kiyosaki is a fantastic example of someone who continued to get back up over and over again. Kiyosaki is the author of Rich Dad Poor Dad, which has sold thirty-two million copies worldwide. Would you believe that his first two companies actually went bankrupt?[19] It didn't matter how many times he failed. Kiyosaki found something deep inside of him to keep going and try again. Talk about a belief that your success is inevitable.

Another one of my favorite perseverance stories is Oprah Winfrey. When Oprah was in her twenties, she was told she was unfit for television news because she was too emotionally invested in her stories.[20] Ladies, we're talking about one of the most successful humans in the world, regardless of gender.

What would have happened if Oprah didn't have that persistence to keep going, even when she was told she wasn't good enough? What I especially love about this story is how Oprah used the exact thing that was supposed to be a limitation, her ability to connect deeply with others, as her biggest superpower, which fueled her immense success.

---

19 (Famous Entrepreneurs, 2019)
20 (Inc.com, 2019)

It doesn't matter how long it takes. It doesn't matter how many times you are told no. The only thing that matters is how badly you want it. How long are you willing to persevere to make your dream a reality?

You can't put a time limit on your dreams. Sometimes they take way longer than you would like them to. Sometimes they are filled with way more failure than you expected. But the truth is none of that matters because your dreams are worth it.

While I still believe in setting deadlines for your goals so you can work backwards to create a plan, you must be flexible on those deadlines. If you give up every time you don't hit a goal by the deadline you set, you will likely never achieve anything.

THE GIFT OF FAILURE

Whenever you set a goal, one of two things happens: you either achieve the goal or you learn a lesson that is necessary to prepare you to achieve an even bigger goal in the future.

When I finally understood this concept, I began to embrace failure with open arms. How many times have you looked at your shortcomings and felt immense gratitude for each of the lessons you learned?

When we actually learn the lessons the universe has sent us, we decrease the total time it takes to achieve our dreams. Therefore, if you really want to hit those milestones faster, the best way to do so is by welcoming failure. As Thomas Watson said, "If you want to increase your success rate, double your failure rate."

On the contrary, when we fail to learn the lessons the universe attempts to send us, it continues to send us the same lesson over and over again, each time with an even bigger impact. For example, one lesson the universe sent me over and over again was the importance of being on time. Each time it attempted to send me this lesson, I was late for something important.

I always picture the universe saying something like, "Well, she didn't learn the lesson. Let's send her an even bigger lesson! This time we're going to make her late for the most important meeting she has ever had!" Finally, it hit me that I needed to learn this lesson so the universe would stop sending it to me.

You may be nodding your head agreeing with me, yet still wondering how you can actually implement this into your life. It sounds nice in theory, but we both know that when you fall short on a goal, it really freaking sucks.

Most people are not in the mood to ask themselves what lessons they have learned when they are in the midst of a failure. This is why, as a part of my daily morning routine, I reflect and journal on any new lessons learned. You would be surprised how many mini failures you have and thus, lessons you learn, on a daily basis.

I follow a simple three step process.

1. What failures did I have yesterday?
2. What was the lesson from each of those failures?
3. What changes am I making today based on those lessons?

By choosing to make this practice a part of your daily routine, you are ensuring that you learn the lessons necessary to keep you moving towards your dreams quickly and efficiently.

But Jaclyn, I don't fail every single day. This process seems excessive.

Real talk, if you are not failing every single day, you're not taking enough risks. This means you're not pushing yourself out of your comfort zone on a daily basis, and it's time to change that. Remember, failure is a good thing. And I don't know about you, but whenever I see a good thing, I always seek more of it!

Your daily failures don't have to be big, crazy goals. Somedays, your failure might be not finishing your to-do list. What's the lesson? You had too many priorities. Other days, your failure may have been not being confident enough on a sales call. What's the lesson? You need to do the inner work to build your confidence in order for your business to be successful.

Before you implement, I challenge you to do an honest assessment of how bad your fear of failure is. On a scale of one to ten, one being no fear at all and ten being debilitating fear, how would you rate yourself?

Here are a few questions to guide your thought process:

- Do you constantly wait until you are "ready" to launch new products, services and ideas?
- Do you worry about what other people will think if you fall short on a goal?
- Do you feel like everything needs to be "perfect" in order for you share it with the world?

If you answered yes to any of those questions, the fear of failure is holding you back from reaching your full potential. If this is the case, the good news is you already have everything you need inside of you to overcome this fear. Below are a few exercises that will aid you in this process:

1. Publicly declare your ninety-day goal to friends and family members. This will help you stop "waiting" until you are ready to spring into action, as well as face the fear of what other people think.

2. Think about the worst thing that could possibly happen if you fall short on your goal. Acknowledge that you can always try again, and there is always a way out of even the worst-case scenario. As Marie Forleo says, "Everything is figureoutable."

3. Go for something BIG that you know you will most likely fail at. Give it your all and acknowledge that failure isn't as bad as you think it is.

DETACHING FROM THE OUTCOME

Gabby Bernstein, best-selling author of *The Universe Has Your Back* explains, "When you're attached to an outcome, you actually block your ability to manifest your desires and co-create with the Universe."[21]

The reason we become attached to an outcome is because we've assumed that when we achieve that outcome, we will be "happy." The problem with this mindset is that, unless you are happy with where you are today, you will never get to where you want to be.

---

21 (Bernstein, 2016)

If you ever think "I'll be happy when when..." you are attached to an outcome. Not only does this block your ability to actually manifest your desires, but it also sets you up to be unhappy when you actually have the thing you want so bad. When I was single, I used to think, "I'll be happy when I'm in a relationship." Then, when I was building my business, I thought "I'll be happy when my business is successful."

Somewhere along the way I learned to be happy today, in this exact moment. Though I have big goals, it is more than possible to work towards them while simultaneously being happy with where I am today. If you find yourself falling into this limited way of thinking, focus on detaching yourself from the outcome of your goals.

Attachment focuses on scarcity and lack. It sets you up to believe that if you don't hit your goal, everything else will fall apart. If you truly believe your success is inevitable, detaching from the outcome should be easy. If you fall short on a goal, you know it's no big deal because you have 100 percent certainty that you'll hit your goal (or an even better goal) in the future.

Of course, like many things in life, this is easier said than done. Below are a few tips I have for learning to detach from the outcome of your goals.

1. Recognize that if you are so attached to a goal, it doesn't allow for you to listen to what's working and change course. If you can't update your strategies and goals based on what you've learned, all chances of success go out the door!

2. Let go of your need for security. Deepak Chopra explains, "Those who seek security in the exterior world chase it for a lifetime. By letting go of your attachment to the illusion of security, which is really an attachment to the known, you step into the field of all possibilities. This is where you will find true happiness, abundance, and fulfillment."

3. Practice meditation to help develop feelings of peace and acceptance for where you are today in your journey.

4. Use affirmations to remind yourself that "you are always on the right path," meaning that wherever you are, you are meant to be in that exact place—whether that place is filled with success or failure.

5. Understand that you will be okay if you don't achieve your goal. Whatever stories you made up in your head about what will happen if you don't hit this specific outcome are probably exaggerated.

6. Appreciate every small achievement that gets you closer to your goal. If your goal is to have a $10,000 month, appreciate every single dollar that comes into your business, knowing although it is getting you closer to your goal, you will be thankful for that dollar regardless of whether or not you hit the specific outcome goal you set.

Often times my clients wonder why we set goals in the first place, if we detach from the outcomes anyway. What they don't realize is how critical goal setting is for success. Without goals, the universe doesn't know where to send us, because it doesn't know where we want to go.

It's like when you secretly want your significant other to have dinner ready for you when you get home from work, but you don't tell him or her, so you arrive home disappointed. How can we expect to receive something, whether from a loved one or the universe, without first asking for it?

**HOW TO APPLY THIS CHAPTER TO YOUR LIFE
TODAY:**

1. Give yourself the virtue of patience in your business. Your dreams are worth waiting for.
2. Journal on new lessons learned from failure on a daily basis.
3. Practice detaching from the outcome of your ninety-day goal.

PART 2:

ACTION

CHAPTER 6:

STOP BEING AFRAID TO INVEST IN YOURSELF

———

Sitting in a brightly lit ballroom at a country club in Blue Bell, Pennsylvania, I was completely mind-blown with all I had learned from working with a business coach for just one day. I couldn't even imagine how much I would learn if I decided to invest in a yearlong coaching program.

My whole body was shaking as I was considering the $15,000 investment. Even though I was fully confident this program would help me take my business to the next level, I couldn't help but question the large investment.

What could I do with $15,000? That's a heck of a lot of money. I could buy a car or save it for a down payment on a house.

I could take my family on a fancy vacation or pay off student loan debt. Why the heck would I spend it on a business coach? Wasn't I smart enough to figure this out on my own? I thought to myself.

Have you ever felt your intuition speak to you? It's sort of like a voice in your head that says something to the extent of: "You need to do this even though you are scared."

As soon as I heard the voice, I knew I had no choice. This guidance was exactly what I needed to grow the business I had always dreamed of. And if I ignored the voice, I knew I would later regret it.

At the time, I had a $5,000 credit limit so there was no way I could put $15,000 on my card. I couldn't write a check because I didn't actually have the money, but I knew I HAD to find a way. So, I did the only thing I could think to do. I asked if I could pay monthly on my credit card.

I was feeling good, until I realized I was actually about to make this super scary decision. That's when the fear kicked in.

Was I really going to go through with this? What if I don't make my money back? Then it hit me—I'm the one in the driver's seat. It is up to me to take full responsibility for taking action and implementing what I learn. And when I do, I just know I'll be successful.

I felt it deep inside my gut. They say trust your gut for a reason—it's usually right. Mine sure was.

**

Three months later I logged into my QuickBooks to see $45,000 in additional revenue in my business. I felt immense joy and pride in my accomplishment. A sea of calm came over my whole body, knowing every single penny was more than worth it. I earned a 300 percent return on my investment in just a few months. Looking back, making that decision should have been a no brainer. I can't even believe I hesitated, but I am thankful I trusted my intuition even when I was afraid.

The world of social media encourages you to "be fearless." While I love my girl Taylor Swift, being fearless is actually unrealistic. We all have fears. We are human beings. We can't turn them off. But here's what we can do: we can choose to take action in spite of our fears. And that, my friend, is the gold secret to pushing the boundaries and achieving even more than you once thought was possible.

THE REAL TRANSFORMATION

James Wedmore says, "The transformation is in the transaction."

I couldn't agree more with this powerful statement. When I invested $15,000 in my business, something funny happened. Before I learned a single thing from my coach, I started to make changes in my business. I became more focused on driving revenue than I ever had been in the past. I made a deep commitment to changing my business and achieving success because of the investment I had made.

This same theory holds true for many of my clients. Often times, before we meet for our first session, I see posts in our Facebook group about major breakthroughs they already have had in the few days it's been since they signed up for my program.

When we make a financial investment in ourselves, we commit to doing the work and making necessary changes to achieve our goals. That commitment makes all the difference when it comes to our success.

Why do we feel so committed? Most people feel like once they invest a large amount of money, there is no turning back. They have to do what it takes to get the maximum value out of this investment. They become determined to see an ROI.

They've already spent the money, so there is nowhere else to turn. This concept is often known as "burning your boats" and is traced back to the conquest of the Aztec Empire in Mexico by Hernan Cortés in 1519.[22]

Cortés and his soldiers sailed from Cuba to Veracruz, Mexico. When they arrived in Mexico, Cortés gathered his soldiers and gave them orders to burn all of the boats they had traveled to Veracruz on. He explained there was no turning back now. They would either win or they would die trying.

The concept in itself is genius. It's easy to retreat when you have the option. You're much less likely to turn back when there is no road behind you. That's because you don't have much of a choice. The only way to go is forward, so forward you will go.

Most people keep their boats as a safety net. The goal of a safety net is to protect you from pain. However, the pain you end up enduring, knowing you gave up on your goal, is significantly worse than the pain of falling flat on your face when you gave it your all.

The concept of burning your boats is something I often implement in my own business. It has propelled me to new

22 (Recruiter, 2019)

heights—heights I probably would have ran from out of fear, if my boats were still there. I highly recommend you learn to embrace this concept in your business to break out of your comfort zone and achieve new levels of success.

Here are a few examples of ways you can do this:

- Invest in your business before you have the money to pay the bills, knowing the investment will bring in much more revenue than you spent
- Commit to something you're not fully prepared for yet, but you know it will move you closer to your goals (like a speech you haven't written yet).
- When you're close to hiring your first employee, rent an office space with two desks, knowing you will soon be filling the extra one.

INFLUENCE OF LIKE-MINDED PEOPLE

As Jim Rohn very famously said, "You are the average of the five people you spend the most time with."[23]

I know, you've heard this a million times before. But if you're anything like 95 percent of people, you've probably heard it and haven't done anything about it.

---

23   (Medium, 2019)

Today, that changes. Because today, you accept full responsibility for the success of your business. And you know if you want to be a six – or seven-figure entrepreneur, you should be hanging out with other six – or seven – figure entrepreneurs.

But Jaclyn, how the heck am I supposed to become friends with six – or seven-figure entrepreneurs? Well, the easiest way is to hire a coach who is a six – or seven-figure entrepreneur. My first three business coaches were all seven-figure entrepreneurs because I was determined to build a multiple seven-figure business. I can confidently say that, because I invested in those coaches, I am well on my way! And you can be, too. But you have to let go of the fear that has been holding you back.

Another great way to build your network is to work with a coach in a group coaching or mastermind format. The other people who have decided to invest in themselves and are also in that group with you are definitely the entrepreneurs you'll want to hang out with.

But Jaclyn, I really don't have any money to invest in a coach or mastermind program. Okay, how about creating your own mastermind? Go to a few local meetups, find other like-minded women, and meet weekly to talk about goals, ideas, and accountability.

It's also incredibly helpful to be surrounded by a community of people who are in a similar stage in their business. Entrepreneurship can get quite lonely. It's nice to have people in your corner who "get it." For this reason, I recommend you get involved in networking groups, especially ones that are filled with your type of people. One of my personal favorite networking groups is called Polka Dot Powerhouse, and I would highly recommend you consider joining if you have a chapter nearby.

Go to conferences and events where other successful entrepreneurs hang out. Who can you connect with? How can you build a relationship with them outside of this event? Begin to get comfortable being uncomfortable because, often times, networking is uncomfortable, but it's so worth that short-lived discomfort.

As Porter Gale says, "Your network is your net worth."[24] I have personally seen the power of my network increasing my net worth many times. Just a few months ago, my friend Haley, who I originally met through an introduction from a mutual connection, introduced me to a college entrepreneurship center where she recently gave her keynote speech. A few weeks later, they booked me as their next keynote speaker on campus.

---

24 (Gale, 2013)

This is just one example of how your network can be incredibly helpful in building your business. If you learn one thing about networking from this chapter, remember to always give before you get. According to the Law of Reciprocity, the more you give, the more you will receive.

WHERE TO START

"Start where you are."

—ARTHUR ASHE[25]

If you are new to investing in yourself, it's okay to start small. In fact, it's more than okay. It's a great place to start!

How about buying a few new books you've been wanting to read for a while? (Props to you for buying this one!) Or what about signing up for that online course that sparks your curiosity? Maybe consider purchasing a ticket to that conference you've been dying to attend.

If you feel anxious about investing in yourself, I encourage you to turn inward and again look at your money mindset. When you breathe out, are you ever worried there won't be enough air to breathe in? Probably not. Your relationship

---

25   (BrainyQuote, 2019)

with money should be the same way. You should be able to let money out without any fear because you know more is already on its way back to you.

Please note that investing in yourself isn't about signing up for any random course or coaching program out there. It doesn't mean jump at the first Facebook ad you see. Rather, it's about investing in opportunities that feel 100 percent in alignment with who you are and where you are going. Simply put, when it's the right fit for you and your future, you will know. And when you know, make sure you find a way to make it happen.

Keep in mind this growth oriented outlook takes time to build. I recommend you consume motivational or education content related to your business growth, money mindset, and personal development at least once a day, if not three to four times a day. Generally, I read in the morning and I listen to a podcast on my way to my office. I listen to another podcast on my way home from my office and I read before bed. Everything I consume inspires me or challenges me to think in a new and better way.

If you are 100 percent committed to your business success, you must also be 100 percent committed to lifelong learning. You can always learn more and you can always step into an even better version of yourself.

Remember, you first need to be the person who does the things that the six – or seven-figure entrepreneur does. Only after this will you see the results in your life. How much time are you committing on a daily basis to work on your mindset? What courses, coaching programs, or conference tickets do you plan on purchasing this year?

One affirmation that has helped me build the confidence to invest in my business is "Every dollar I invest in my business comes back to me multiplied." Whenever I feel nervous to make an investment, I repeat this to myself over and over again. It's a great reminder that investing in your business will help you generate more money and even greater success.

All successful entrepreneurs invest in themselves. The more you invest in yourself, the more you will grow. So, start today, wherever you are—even if it's only a ten-dollar book. You don't need to buy a $15,000 coaching program, but you do need to start somewhere.

HOW TO APPLY THIS CHAPTER TO YOUR LIFE TODAY:

1. Make a financial investment in your business that scares you.
2. Start spending time with entrepreneurs who are doing the things you want to do.
3. Join a networking group or community with like-minded women.
4. If you're scared to invest in yourself, start small—buy a book, conference ticket, or online course.

CHAPTER 7:

STOP WAITING UNTIL YOU ARE READY

———

I wasn't ready to write this book. In fact, I re-wrote it three times. They do say third time's a charm!

I literally wrote the whole book and then, as I began to edit it, I felt like it wasn't good enough. Instead of continuing to edit it to make it better like most normal people would do, I decided to start from scratch…twice.

I scrapped every word I had poured my heart and soul into because my manuscripts didn't live up to my unrealistic standard of perfection. I even pushed back the publishing date one month because I was so caught up in doing whatever I could to make sure my manuscript was flawless.

Have you ever done anything like that in your business? Did you put off launching something that was filled with awesome content because you were stuck living up to impossible, self-imposed standards?

Finally, my publisher gave me a strict deadline. If I wanted my book to be published, I needed to submit it to copyediting within thirty days.

And then I realized I was doing the exact thing I teach my clients not to do. Funny how that works, isn't it?

After I talked with my publishing company about the deadline, I committed myself to moving forward, giving it my all, and trusting the value I knew was inside of me. And guess what—it worked! Once I gave myself permission to write from my heart and be imperfectly perfect, the words started to flow from out of me quicker than ever. By the time I finished writing, I knew this book was going to change lives.

As an entrepreneur, everything you create is deeply linked to your personal value. You feel like you can't let go of things until they are perfect because, if they are not, it means you are not perfect.

I'm going to break this limiting belief for you once and for all. Guess what? You're not perfect. No one is perfect. We are all imperfect human beings, and our imperfection is what makes us shine. Do you think you would have been able to relate to me if every story I told was about how perfect my business is? Of course not!

The imperfection in your work makes you relatable and enables you to help people. Your work doesn't need to be perfect. And if you wait until it's perfect, you're actually being pretty selfish because there are people out there who desperately it.

As Sheryl Sandberg says, "Done is better than perfect."[26]

YOU WILL NEVER BE READY

Let's be honest, have you ever felt truly ready for anything in your life? I wasn't ready to graduate high school or college. I wasn't ready to start my business. I wasn't ready to invest in my business, write my books, or launch my coaching programs. I've never been ready.

The secret to taking action before you're ready isn't as complicated as you might think. All you need to do is fully accept the fact that you will never be ready, and if you wait until you are, you will spend your whole life waiting. Unless you

---

26 (Goodreads.com, 2019)

want to look back on your life at ninety years old in a nursing home thinking, "I wish I pushed myself out of my comfort zone and took more risks," there is no better time to pursue your dreams than the present.

As Hugh Laurie says, "It's a terrible thing, I think, in life to wait until you're ready. I have this feeling now that actually no one is ever ready to do anything. There is almost no such thing as ready. There is only now. And you may as well do it now. Generally speaking, now is as good a time as any."

The only way you will achieve the success you desire is through action. Waiting until you are ready is just another example of how you are getting in your own way. Because without action, there is no failure. And without failure, there are no lessons. And without lessons, there is no progress. And without progress, you stay stuck exactly where you are.

So unless you want to stay in the exact same spot as you are in today, it's time you start doing something about it!

Of course, like many of the things we've talked about in this book, taking action is always easier said than done. Below are the steps I take to help make the process of springing into action easy, effortless, and fun:

1. Create a ninety-day action plan that aligns with your ninety-day goal.
2. Focus on revenue-driving activities. Seeing money flow into your bank account as a result of your action steps is incredibly motivating.
3. Optimize your work environment. Do you like to work from home? An office? A coffee shop?
4. Consume inspirational content before you start your day. We all need a daily dose of motivation, no matter how self-motivated we are.
5. Start your day with the most important activity. Ask yourself, "If I could only get done one task today to move me closer to my ninety-day goal, what would it be?"
6. If you're unsure what action steps to take, seek the expertise of coaches, experts, and mentors who have already accomplished the exact things you want to accomplish—there is no need to reinvent the wheel.

THE PATH TO CLARITY

"Clarity comes from action, not thought."

—MARIE FORLEO[27]

I used to think if I could simply figure out the answer in my head, I would implement it and everything would be perfect.

---

27 (Goodreads.com, 2019)

Naturally, things didn't work out that way. I quickly learned that no matter how much planning I did, something would always come up that I didn't plan for.

By taking action, I learned exactly what I like and what I don't like. I learned I prefer to work from an office rather than from home. I learned I enjoy teaching business growth strategies and mindset development much more than sales scripts or marketing funnels.

I learned my audience is seeking actionable steps to grow their specific business, and they are not interested in learning generic advice about growing their business. I learned some of my followers prefer my content at a lower price point in a DIY format, whereas others would like my support every step of the way. I learned I don't like having launches every month. I'd prefer to actually have time to spend with my current clients.

Because of these learnings, I've built a business that is rooted in both what I love and what my clients need. If this model speaks to you, and you'd like to design your business in a similar way, all you need to do is take action.

Let's say you are deciding what content you want to cover in your online course. You are passionate about two topics and you don't know which is a better choice. You can think about the two topics as much as you'd like, but your true clarity will come when you pick one and launch it.

Did your audience respond well to the topic? Did you enjoy teaching it? The only way to find the answers to these questions, and thus give you the clarity you are seeking, is to take action.

Often times it's not the action steps themselves that either work or don't work, it's the way you implement them. For example, if you follow a specific email campaign strategy and it doesn't work, it could be the strategy itself or it could be that the copy didn't resonate with your target audience. So much testing needs to be done to ensure you have the right messaging for your audience. The longer you wait to launch, the more time you'll have to spend in the future figuring it out. To reduce that timeline, simply start as soon as possible.

Whatever you are seeking clarity on today, I challenge you to choose to take action, knowing those action steps will bring you the clarity you've been seeking.

SPIRITUAL GUIDANCE

While I have always been a spiritual person, it took me quite a while to understand the connection between spirituality and business. Traditionally, we are taught the two don't mesh.

Contrary to popular belief, the real magic didn't start happening until I meshed the two. Spirituality has been one of the main reasons I am able to propel myself into action without letting fear hold me back.

My introduction to spirituality in business came from Gabrielle Bernstein in her book, *The Universe Has Your Back: Transform Fear to Faith*.[28] Gabby introduced me to the idea that the universe communicates with us through signs.

We all have our own sign. It could be a number, a symbol, an animal, or an object. How do you know what your sign is? Quite simply, it will come to you. If you don't yet know what your sign is, what comes to mind when reading this? If something immediately pops into your head—trust it. That is your sign.

If you feel unsure, trust that the universe will reveal your sign to you soon. When I was reading The Universe Has Your Back, I immediately knew my sign was a butterfly.

But here's the funny thing—I never saw butterflies. The only butterflies I saw that whole year were on a pair socks my mom gave me for Christmas (because I told her they were my sign).

---

28 (Bernstein, 2016)

At the time, I was running my first business, a health and wellness company I started while I was in college. About two years into that business, I began to question what was next for me. I felt I made a positive impact and was ready for something bigger. But, like most people, I was held back by fear.

Imagine pouring your heart and soul into something for two years and then thinking, maybe I want to start a different business. I was questioning myself and my "purpose" on so many levels.

Was I making a mistake? Or was I being called to help female entrepreneurs for a reason?

These questions were coming from fear because I was afraid to leave my comfort zone. But here's the funny thing about comfort zones: they're not actually comfortable. Heather Monahan, author of Confidence Creator, explains it's really just a "familiar zone."

I was far from comfortable in this place of deep soul searching. I felt lost, confused, and uninspired.

This is when I was introduced to angel numbers. I heard the concept for the first time on Kathrin Zenkina's Manifestation Babe podcast and thought, well at this point I'm pretty desperate for guidance so it can't hurt to keep my eyes out for these "angel number things."[29]

If you're wondering what the heck these "angel number things" are, they're combinations of repeating and sequential numbers that the universe uses to communicate with us. I like to think of them as a way for my loved ones who are no longer with me to guide me through life.

The most common angel numbers are three or more repeating digits. So, for example 000, 111, 222, etc. Each combination has its own specific meaning that your angels are trying to communicate with you.

I was listening to Kathrin's podcast as I was driving to my office one morning. And then something really freaking weird happened. I drove by a gas station that said gas was $9.99 per gallon on its big lit-up sign.

This was in Pennsylvania where it's rare that gas is ever more than three dollars a gallon. Seeing $9.99 is literally unheard of.

Now I was getting freaked out. What does 999 mean? As soon as I parked, I opened Google and started researching the meaning of 999.

---

29 (Zenkina, 2019)

Trustedpsychicmediums.com says, "The angel number 999 indicates you are closing a major chapter and moving towards something new. You are leaving something behind and looking forward to receiving something new."[30]

And in that moment, I knew there was no reason to hold onto any fear. I was being called to this new journey. It was time to close the chapter and open a new one. It was okay to let go of my first business. The next day, I opened the doors to Clarity and Action Consulting so I could fulfill a deep passion inside of me to help female entrepreneurs achieve their biggest dreams.

Guess what happened once I made that decision? Butterflies started to appear everywhere. Often times, I'd be sitting on the beach, and a butterfly would land on my arm and simply sit there, flapping its beautiful wings. Everyone around me would talk about how weird it was that butterflies were constantly landing on me because they had never seen anything like it.

With a deep sense of relief and a big smile, I thanked the universe for reminding me I was on the right path and I kept moving towards my new goals.

---

30 (Freeman, 2019)

And it didn't stop there. I constantly see angel numbers and butterflies everywhere I go. These help me make decisions in my business as well as pick up my spirits when I've been putting in a lot of work without seeing results. Now that I am fully in tune with my spirituality and the ways the universe communicates with me, I rarely feel lost. I know I am always being guided and therefore, am always on the right path. It's incredibly freeing to fully step into this belief because it allows you to let go of any fears you've been holding onto.

If you ever feel lost or wonder if you're moving in the right direction, I highly recommend you start to be aware of angel numbers and your sign. Opening your heart to spirituality in your business opens the doors to a new level of success that pushes the boundaries of what you once thought was possible.

HOW TO APPLY THIS CHAPTER TO YOUR LIFE TODAY:

1. Repeat the affirmation "done is better than perfect" anytime you fall into inaction as a result of perfectionism.
2. Take action on the one thing you are currently seeking clarity on.
3. Begin to look for angel numbers and your sign in daily life.

CHAPTER 8:

STOP WORKING 80-HOUR WEEKS

Something I often heard as a kid was, "If you want to be successful, you have to work hard." So, naturally, I made the assumption that if I want to be more successful, I have to work harder.

Tim Notke said, "Hard work beats talent when talent doesn't work hard." While I do believe in the power of hard work and agree that building a business does require hard work, this quote actually did me more harm than good.[31]

---

31   (Goodreads.com, 2019)

I assumed if I could just work harder than anyone else, I could be more successful than anyone else. This theory proved itself to be true in school. I always studied longer and harder than my classmates and, internally, I attributed my academic success to hard work. While hard work played a big role, I was also smart, attentive, and committed. I failed to realize hard work wasn't the only reason for my success.

When I started my business, I held onto this same mentality. If I could just work more hours than anyone else, my business would be more successful than any of its competitors. This led me into a cycle of working long hours followed by periods of burnout. Not only was this unhealthy, but it was also incredibly counterproductive for my business.

I remember many mornings I would wake up after a full nights' sleep and my whole body would feel heavy. Even though I had passion for my business, I was quite simply tired of working so many hours. During these periods, I did my best to "work," but I often found myself distracted and exhausted. I would have been better off giving it my all for a forty-hour week than half-assing an eighty-hour week.

Who said in order to be successful you have to work eighty-hour weeks? What if, instead, we capped our work weeks at a maximum of forty hours? How focused would you be during those precious forty hours?

I firmly believe you can achieve massive levels of success without working crazy hours. In fact, according to the Be Do Have Model, the most important time in your day is the time you dedicate to becoming the version of you who does the things the person you want to be does and, thus, has the things you want to have. If you're spending 80 hours a week working, when are you growing? When are you reading books about personal and business development? When are you repeating your affirmations? When are you visualizing your champagne moment? When are you exercising so your brain can get the stress relief it needs? Those things are just as important in building a successful business as the time you actually spend working.

So, if you're really committed to making the necessary changes to build the business you've always dreamed of, it's time for you reject the idea that hustle is the answer.

THE TRUTH ABOUT PRODUCTIVITY

Years ago, when my older sister got married and moved out of my parents' house, I was given the privilege of using not only my closet, but the closet in her room, too.

At the time, I didn't really need additional closet space, but I wasn't going to turn down more room for my clothes and shoes. At first, I only filled up a small space in the closet.

Little by little, I found myself accumulating more and more things I really didn't need because I knew I could simply throw it in my sister's closet.

Five years later, my clothes and rarely used items that probably should be thrown away not only take up her whole closet, but the whole room itself. The room is literally overflowing with stuff I simply don't need.

The more space available, the more you find things to fill it. The same concept applies to your time. Parkinson's Law states "work expands to fill the time available for its completion."[32]

If you give yourself eighty hours to complete a task that could be done in forty hours, you end up making the task more complex than it needed to be, so you use the eighty hours you allocated.

I've seen this proven true many times in my professional life. When I was on a deadline for this book, I found a way to finish it in the time I was allocated. We can always "make it work" and, better yet, do a great job when we have a set amount of time in front of us.

---

32 (Lifehack, 2019)

When it's Friday afternoon and I need to finish certain projects by the end of the week, I become super productive and finish my tasks quickly and efficiently. There is something magical about having a limited amount of time to finish a project.

Stanford University professor John Pencavel found in his research that employee output falls sharply after a fifty-hour work week. Not surprisingly, Pencavel found that a person who works seventy hours produces nothing more than a person who works fifty-five hours, meaning the last fifteen hours were a complete waste of time.[33]

Psychologist Ron Friedman found in his research that most people "typically have a window of about three hours where we're really, really focused." RescueTime backed this data with their own study of 225 million hours of working time and found "the average knowledge worker (someone who deals with information for a living, like a writer, developer, designer, or manager), is only productive for 12.5 hours a week. That's roughly 2.5 hours a day."[34]

Working long hours is well-intentioned but, often times, we don't realize the consequences of our well-intentioned

---

33   (Kabir Sehgal, 2019)
34   (RescueTime Blog, 2019)

actions. Working long hours is directly correlated with burnout. When you burnout, not only does your performance suffer but, many times, you are unable to work at all. Studies show that more than 60 percent of work absenteeism is caused by psychological stress and stress-related burnout.[35]

If you want to show up as the best version of yourself, which you absolutely must do every single day to grow your business and achieve your goals, you need to stop working such long hours.

THE POWER OF INTENTION

If you only had, say, two hours to work today, would you focus on something that doesn't matter? Or would you focus on something directly related to your goals?

When we have less time to work, the time we do spend working becomes more intentional.

Wayne Dyer says, "Our intention creates our reality."[36] If you're ready to start spending your days intentionally focused on activities that move you closer to your goals while having

---

35   (Boyd, 2019)
36   (BrainyQuote, 2019)

more free time to spend with loved ones, you're in the right place.

The first step to spending your time more intentionally is to set strict working hours. This has been a game changer for my business. I go to work at the same time every day and I leave work at the same time every day. Unless I have a strict deadline (like I do with this manuscript), I treat these working hours with utmost respect.

The second step to spending your time more intentionally is to focus on your one thing. I recommend entrepreneurs pick just one product or service to focus on. Your audience should be able to easily recall what the one thing you sell is and where they can go to purchase it.

If you try to do too many things, you will do a mediocre job at them all. It's much more efficient to focus on one thing and hit the ball out of the park. Remember your garden from chapter 1? What flower are you choosing to water?

I also recommend you apply the one thing concept to your daily and weekly planning. Pick one output goal for the week. Then pick one task you can complete each day that will keep you on track to your weekly output goal. Though you will obviously do other things throughout the week, even if you only get that one thing done, you will be moving closer toward your big goals, and that's what matters most.

It's best to do your one thing as soon as you start your work-day—that way, if you get distracted by incoming emails or fires you need to put out, you've already accomplished the most important task of your day. It's quite empowering to know that, by 10 a.m., you've already finished the most important task of your day, so even if you did nothing the rest of the day, it would still be a successful day.

Another helpful productivity tip is to time block. If it's important to you in your day, it should be blocked off in your calendar the same way you would block off a client appointment. Once it's blocked off, you should hold that time just as sacred as you actually would hold a client appointment. Unless it's an emergency, nothing should come ahead of that "meeting" you have with yourself to focus on important tasks in your business.

Lastly, I can't urge you enough to focus on revenue-driving activities. Get clear on what you are selling and who you are selling it to. Then, focus on the activities that increase sales. I see so many female entrepreneurs being super "productive," yet at the end of the day their business doesn't make enough money (if it makes any at all).

If your business doesn't make money, you will have to give up your dreams and get a job. So, it you haven't already, it's time to put your product or service out there in the world and spend the majority of your time doing activities that help sell your product or service.

THE IMPORTANCE OF BUILDING A TEAM

Another great way to increase output without increasing the hours you work is to build a team. Usually, when I mention this to my clients, I can literally see the anxiety come over their body.

But Jaclyn, I can't afford a team. I can barely afford to pay myself. How can you expect me to hire other people? I want to let you in on a little secret. No one feels ready to hire their first employee. No matter who you are, hiring your first employee is really freaking scary. But you already know you can't wait until you feel ready because that day will never come.

Just like I recommended when we discussed investing in yourself, follow Arthur Ashe's advice and "start where you are."[37]

---

37   (BrainyQuote, 2019)

My first ever team members were unpaid interns. I remembered how difficult it was for me to land internships in college, so I figured I would give it a try. I posted on my Instagram about the internship opportunity and had eleven applicants in the first twenty-four hours.

Need administrative help? Hire a virtual assistant. There are many virtual assistants in the Philippines who charge three dollars an hour. For just fifteen dollars a week, you could get five hours of your precious time back. And, if you've followed the above steps, those five hours could go toward intentional activities that move you closer to your goals. How powerful is that?

If you're not sure what tasks to outsource, begin to make a list of tasks that can be done by someone else. There are usually two categories on this list. One is tasks that can actually be done better by someone else, like accounting or copywriting. Unless you are an expert it in a specific field, let someone who is do it. It's worth every penny. The other category on the list of tasks that can be done by someone else is repetitive, mundane tasks. These tasks simply aren't worth your time, and a VA can easily take these over.

And guess what happens next? With that five hours per week you freed up, you drive in an additional $20,000 in revenue. Now you're ready to hire your first part-time employee.

As James Wedmore says, "The reason you can't afford to hire anyone is because you haven't actually been hiring anyone."[38]

Whenever my clients bring on their first team member, even if it's a VA, a part-time personal assistant, or an unpaid intern, their first comment is "Why didn't I do this sooner?"

Before you know it, you will be amazed by how quickly your business is growing because you finally freed up your own time to operate in your personal zone of genius. What's your zone of genius? It's the thing you're really good at. When you're operating in your zone of genius, you're doing the activities that actually help grow your business rather than simply run your business.

Your success IS inevitable, and it's time you realize you don't need to do it alone!

---

38   (Wedmore, 2019)

HOW TO APPLY THIS CHAPTER TO YOUR LIFE TODAY:

1. Set strict working hours. What time will you start and end work each day? How many hours will you work each week? Be sure this number is at the very highest, less than fifty-five hours, though I personally recommend forty hours.

2. Spend time each Sunday writing out your one thing for the week and one thing for each day that you will be focusing on.

3. Hire your first team member, even if it's an unpaid intern or VA in the Philippines.

CHAPTER 9:

STOP DOWNPLAYING YOUR BUSINESS

I can't tell you the number of times I've met someone, they asked what I "do," I told them, and I got a response like, "So you don't have a real job?" Or "How do you make money?" Some of my favorite responses of all time include:

"You're a speaker? What does that even mean? Who do you speak to?"

"So you don't have a real job?"

"Aw, that's so cute—you have a little business."

"How inspiring. You can always get a job if it doesn't work out."

And the very best one ever: "I thought entrepreneurs were supposed to be older."

At one point it was so bad I avoided talking about my business as often as I could. Last year, I remember absolutely dreading going to my yearly checkup at the doctor. Every year, my doctor asks me what's new and spends some time catching up with me about my life. When he asked about my career, I quickly said I was doing consulting and changed the subject before he had a chance to get in another word.

If you're anything like I used to be, you probably feel uncomfortable talking about your big goals because most people around you are settling for a far less fulfilling life.

Zig Ziglar said, "Don't let someone who gave up on their dreams talk you out of going after yours."[39]

Let's be honest, most people don't get it. Ninety-five percent of people are afraid to follow their dreams, so to make themselves feel better, they talk down on yours.

You need to realize it's not about you. It's about them. Their reaction is directly related to the way they feel about themselves.

---

39 (Goodreads.com, 2019)

By letting the haters dim my light, I was actually standing in my own way, holding myself back from potential opportunities. What if my doctor's daughter recently started a business and was looking for a mentor? Or, what if he was well connected at a local university and could help me land a speaking gig there?

Believe it or not, most people actually want to help you. It makes them feel good when they make a positive impact on your future. But no one can help you if they don't know you own a business. The first step being confident and embracing your role as an entrepreneur and business owner.

LET GO OF WHAT THEY THINK

"One day the people who didn't believe in you will be telling people how they mwr you."—Johnny Depp[40]

I've found a funny phenomenon with this one. The longer I've been in business and the more success I've had, the more people ask me about it.

I find many people in my life couldn't care less what I was doing a few years ago, but now that they see my flying across

---

40 (Goodreads.com, 2019)

the country for speaking gigs, they are all of a sudden interested in what I'm doing.

Why is this important? Because your success will speak for itself. You don't need to prove yourself to anyone. Keep your head down, stay in your lane, and let your many accolades and achievements that are coming in the near future quiet the noise. There is no need to argue or defend yourself, especially to someone whose opinion doesn't matter, because, soon enough, they will have no choice but to admit how incredibly successful you are.

As Steve Martin says, "Be so good they can't ignore you."[41]

If you allow yourself run to your business from a place of fear due to the opinions of other people, your business is destined to fail. What do you want more: a successful company or the acceptance of a distant relative you talk to twice a year?

If you are fully committed to your business success, you need to learn to ignore the noise. Or better yet, use it as inspiration to prove them wrong. Think of all the people who didn't get it and all the people who wondered how you were making money or why you didn't want to work a regular job. What are they going to say when you're interviewed on Good

---

41 (Business Insider, 2019)

Morning America? What are they going to say when your book is #1 on the New York Times Best Seller list?

It doesn't matter what they think of you. The only thing that matters is what you think of you because what you think of you physically manifests into your reality.

If you're totally on board with ditching the opinions of others but still having trouble with how to actually stop caring, here are a few tangible tips.

- Start trying small exercises that push you out of your comfort zone in order to let go of the fear of what people think. For example, go out to dinner without makeup on or go grocery shopping in your pajamas. These small acts will begin to build your confidence muscle, which helps you let go of the opinions of others.
- Surround yourself with friends who make decisions based on what's best for them rather than what other people think. It makes it easier to put yourself first when you're surrounded by others who are doing the same.
- Take a freezing cold shower or run one mile longer than you think you can. This is all about proving to yourself that you can do hard things. Silencing your inner mean girl isn't as hard as you think because you are a total badass. Repeat these exercises anytime you feel like the

voice in your head is bulling you into caring what other people think.

- Do it for the little girl you once were. Think back to when you were five years old and it didn't matter if you were wearing a princess costume when everyone else was wearing jeans. You couldn't have cared less what other people were doing or what they thought of you. That girl is still inside of you somewhere. You just need to bring her out!

TELL EVERYONE

The more people who know about your business, the more potential customers you will have, the more press you will land, and the more social media followers you will have.

The more people who know about your business, the better. If you've constantly been downplaying your business, it's time to get out of your comfort zone and step into the attention your business deserves.

Starting now, you will tell every new person you meet about your business. If this makes you uncomfortable, that's a good sign. Most of the magic happens just outside your comfort zone. And here's the best part: it won't be as scary as you think it will be. All you need is some practice.

Remember the first time you went on a date? I remember mine clear as day. I was sixteen years old and I went to the movies with a boy I had a huge crush on, Richie (who just so happens to be my fiancé).

Even though I was dying to go on a date with Richie, I was nervous because I didn't have any experience. I remember sitting on my bed a few hours before the date wondering if I should even go in the first place. Butterflies filled my stomach as I picked out my outfit and put on my makeup.

After the movie, Richie dropped me off at my house. The whole car ride home, all I could think about was whether or not he was going to try to kiss me. I was so nervous I jumped out of the car before he even had a chance to make a move.

As you may have guessed, the date was super awkward, which is probably why he didn't ask me on another one. After the date, we remained friends, seeing each other occasionally.

Four years later, Richie asked me on our second first date. This time, I was less nervous. I now had been on many dates over the years. I finally had that practice I lacked on our first date, and that practice gave me confidence.

Telling others about your business is just like going on dates. The first time you do it, you will probably be super awkward. But that's totally okay because it's the first step in building your confidence. The more you do it, the more comfortable you will feel. And, eventually, you won't think twice about telling everyone you meet about the awesome business you started.

If the idea of telling every new person you meet about your business feels unrealistic for you, start small. Why not tell just one new person per week about your business? Then, increase that to three new people per week and eventually one new person every day.

STOP UNDERVALUING YOURSELF

The same people who downplay their business also downplay their prices, meaning they don't charge enough money for their products and services.

Although I don't know anything about your business specifically, I do know a thing or two about female entrepreneurs. And one of the most common problems I see in female founders run into is pricing their products or services too low.

Thus, my first piece of advice for you is to raise your prices. You are probably undervaluing yourself or your products.

I learned this pricing lesson when I was running a Kickstarter campaign to get my first business off the ground. I had a goal of raising $20,000, and if you've ever used Kickstarter, you know unless you raise all of the money, you don't get any of it.

I was about two weeks into my campaign and I had raised $10,000. It was thirty day campaign, so I had about two weeks left to raise the final $10,000. This may have sounded easy, since I previously raised that amount, but I had already asked everyone in my network to support my campaign, so I didn't know where to turn for the final $10,000.

One day, while I was at working out my school gym, I had an idea. I looked around and saw hundreds of students going in and out of the gym during the short thirty minutes I was there. Georgetown had thousands of students. What if I asked each student to pledge just one dollar toward my campaign? I figured I would be willing to give one dollar to a fellow student, so I was sure most students would be willing to give one dollar to me.

After trying this strategy for a few days, I had raised an additional $300. I still had a long way to go to $10,000. So, I sought out the advice of my professor and mentor, Eric Koester. When I told Eric about my new strategy, he responded with, "Jaclyn, do you think it would be easier to get 10,000 people to pledge one dollar or ten people to pledge $1,000?"

"Hm...I never thought about it that way," I responded.

This sparked a lot of thought. I was doing way more work than necessary. All I needed was to find ten people who

I could sell my $1,000 package too, which included a corporate lunch and learn. I began to ask everyone in my network if their companies were interested in this package and, before I knew it, I broke the $20,000 mark on my campaign.

When you are pricing your products and services, make sure your price point aligns with your income goals. If your goal is one million dollars in revenue and you are selling a hundred-dollar online course, you need to sell your course to 10,000 people to hit your income goal. This isn't realistic for most people, unless you have a huge audience. However, if you instead sold a $1,000 course, you now only need to sell it to 1,000 people. Or, if you decided to offer a $10,000 coaching program, you would only need one hundred people in that program to hit your one million-dollar goal.

Next, I recommend you do the mindset work to see the incredible value in your offerings. One exercise that has helped me and many of my clients is something I call "Fifteen Reasons." In this exercise, write down fifteen reasons why your product or service is worth every penny. Then, read your fifteen reasons over and over again until you truly believe your product or service is worth the price you are charging.

You can also apply the fifteen reasons exercise to any area you lack confidence in. I see a lot of women who feel like they don't "deserve" success. If this resonates with you, make a list of fifteen reasons why you deserve success. If you feel like you're not "qualified enough" to teach what your content, write down a list of fifteen reasons why you are highly qualified.

If you still don't see the value in your product or service, ask yourself if there is anything else you can include to increase its value. For example, maybe you include weekly Q&A sessions with your online course so each of your clients can get the one-on-one attention they may need to succeed.

Remember, your time is your most valuable asset. If you're ready to build your dream business, you need to start valuing it!

Remember we talked about how my biggest transformations came from large financial investments I made in myself? So much of my transformations were in the commitment I made to myself by spending that money. The same thing applies to your customers. If you really care about changing lives, one of the best ways you can do this is to pursue a large financial investment. The more committed your customers are to themselves, the more changes they will see in their life.

HOW TO APPLY THIS CHAPTER TO YOUR LIFE TODAY:

1. Use any judgement from others about your business as motivation to prove them wrong.
2. Tell everyone you meet about how awesome your business is.
3. Increase your prices or, at the very least, do an honest assessment of whether or not your prices are too low.

CHAPTER 10:

STOP TRYING TO
CONTROL THE HOW

———

A few years back, I desperately needed a car. Whenever I drove my beat-up, seventeen-year-old Ford Taurus, clouds of smoke would pour out from underneath the hood.

Given the circumstances, I couldn't help but attempt to control the situation. Sure, I wanted to manifest a new car and I knew one of the keys to manifestation is letting go of the "how," but I needed a car...like, yesterday.

So I began to research like crazy. At the time, I had about $4,000 in savings, and most used cars that were relatively new and had low miles on them ranged from $10,000 to $15,000.

I was determined to control the situation. I was going to find myself an affordable car that checked all of my boxes. I spent every free moment I had on Kelley Blue Book researching the value of each car I was interested in.

I even considered buying a new car because the interest rates were so low I knew I wouldn't have a problem making the monthly payments. Still, that felt like a silly choice to me because I didn't want to dig myself into a hole, so I went back to my used car research.

Every time I found a car I thought was the one, I found something wrong with it. Some were stick shift (which I have no idea how to drive), others were involved in major accidents, and some were so old they probably had just as many problems as my Ford Taurus.

After about three weeks of this, I finally threw in the towel. I searched the internet up and down and found no cars met my standards and fell within my price point. I decided I would continue driving my smoky old car until I had at least $10,000 saved.

I made peace with my choice and that night, for the first time in a while, I went to bed stress-free. I knew everything would work out once I saved up a bit more money. I felt I was on the right path.

The next morning, I received a call from my mom. One of the doctors in the office she works at was selling her car. This silver Toyota Prius was previously used by her au pair and had very few miles on it. She wanted to first offer it to her employees at a discounted price before putting it on the market for a stranger.

It's no surprise that her asking price for the car was $4,000 on the dot! You can probably guess what happened next.

I was one happy camper driving home my new wheels. Finally, a car was within my budget and had everything I was looking for. It even had a backup camera, which wasn't on my original list. I actually made out better than I could have possibly planned.

It was no coincidence that when I finally stopped trying to control the how, the universe took care of it for me.

You can manifest anything you want in your life and your business but, before you do, you must first let go of the how.

START SMALL

Let's back up a few steps. If you're new to the woo-woo stuff, manifestation is when something that was once a thought or dream becomes your physical reality.

Throughout this book, we've been talking about manifesting your dream business using both the Law of Attraction and the Law of Action. In order to apply everything you've learned in this book, you must take the final step and let go of the how once and for all.

As a Type A personality, I like to be in control of almost everything. So, when I first tried to let go of the how, I fell flat on my face. I couldn't leave the "how" up to chance—I had to take control of my own life.

The harder I tried to control the how, the more I fell short on my goals. I quickly realized control was not the answer, but I didn't know how I could give it up.

Until one day, I had an idea. What if I tried to manifest something really small and let go of that how? Something that didn't really matter to me much, like a cup of coffee or a front row parking spot. At the time, I was sitting on the beach thinking about how hungry I was.

One of my favorite summertime snacks is my future mother-in-law's buffalo chicken dip. Her recipe is the perfect blend of savory and spicy. It is hands down the best buffalo chicken dip I've ever had.

I began to visualize sitting in the backyard, enjoying every bite of buffalo chicken dip. And then, I committed to letting go of the how. Though I really wanted this buffalo chicken dip, I trusted the universe would take care of me. I knew if I didn't eat buffalo chicken dip, I would eat something else and my hunger would be satisfied. I felt totally detached from the outcome.

When we arrived home from the beach, my future mother-in-law told me she was going to make buffalo chicken dip since dinner wasn't for a few hours. I was overjoyed! I felt like such a girl boss. I did it. I finally let go of the how.

And I have to say, that buffalo chicken dip tasted even better because I knew I manifested it.

Now it's your turn to manifest something small by fully surrendering. Truly let go of the how and trust it will come to you.

TAKE IT A STEP FURTHER

Once you've learned to let go of the how with something small, it's time to apply the same strategy to something bigger.

The first time I did this was at the Women Empower X conference in Washington, D.C. I was a speaker on a panel at the conference, and I decided to spend the day learning from the other speakers who were giving talks at the event. My friend Shannon traveled to D.C. with me for the day so she could learn and be inspired as well. We decided to attend a talk about business finance mostly because they advertised they were giving away a trip to Cancun, and who doesn't want a free trip?

At the beginning of the session, all attendees were asked to fill out a yellow information card, which was then passed up to the front of the room and place into a big basket. All throughout the talk, I began to visualize the moderator pulling my yellow card out of the basket and declaring I was the winner to the audience. I envisioned myself walking up to the front of the room and accepting the free trip.

When the speech was over, the moderator announced it was time for the free trip giveaway. I kept repeating my name to myself inside my head over and over and over again.

I had a feeling deep inside my gut that they were indeed going to pull my name. To prove this, I turned to Shannon right before the drew the winner and said, "They are about to call my name." I didn't want to tell my friend I "knew" they were going to call me after they called my name because who would believe that?

Before Shannon even had a chance to respond, we heard, "And the winner is…Jaclyn DiGregorio."

With my heart beating out of its chest, I ran up to the front of the room and was given an information sheet about the free trip I had just won.

When I returned to my seat, Shannon's jaw was still wide open. "How did you know you were going to win?"

"I manifested it. I felt it in my intuition. I just knew," I explained.

Once I realized how powerful manifestation can be, I decided to apply it to my biggest goals, which, of course, related to my business. I began to reach new heights and milestones that I once would have thought were totally impossible. And here's the special thing—you can do it too.

Set the goal. Do all the mindset work we've talked about, like visualization and affirmations. Take the action steps in your ninety-day plan. Commit to doing the work. And then, let go.

How do you know if you've truly let go? If you've fully surrendered, you won't have any fear of failure. For example, say you invest more money than you currently have in an upcoming launch. If you've truly let go of the how, you will have full confidence that your launch will bring in the money you need to pay your credit card bill because you know the universe has already taken care of it.

Your goal should be to live as if it's already been done. You've already made the money. You already had the successful launch. You've already manifested the house or the car.

How can you build this immense trust? For me, it's twofold. First, I have been able to surrender and make large investments in my business without fear because I know I'm in control of my own actions and I'm committed to always finding a way to make it work. If I can't drive where I want to go because the road is closed, I'll walk. If I have to, I'll dig a hole underground and create a tunnel to get where I'm going. And because of this unwavering commitment to my dreams, it's easier for me to let go of the how. I know it will work out, one way or another, at some point in time, whether it's sooner or later.

Second, I've been able to fully let go of the how by getting in tune with my spirituality.

TRUST THE UNIVERSE

I want you to think back on something in your life that turned out even better than you could have possibly imagined. Then, think about the series of events that led up to that amazing moment.

When I think back on how Richie and I started dating, I can't believe how important every little decision was. As you may remember, we had been friends for years and went on our first date in high school but grew apart in college.

Until, one day, a few of my friends decided they wanted to take a day trip to the Jersey Shore. One of our friends was renting a house for the weekend, so we figured we would spend the day with him on the beach.

It just so happens the house my friend was renting was on the same street as Richie's parents' house. When I walked on the beach and saw Richie, my heart skipped a beat. I couldn't believe he was there. I hadn't seen him in years, and he was cuter than ever.

We started talking, and the rest is history. If you want to listen to our proposal, head over to the Manifestation Babe podcast and listen to episode 112.

I always wonder what would have happened if I decided not to take a day trip to the beach that day. Or, what would have happened if my friend had rented a house on a different street?

But here's the thing: the universe doesn't make mistakes. These were small coincidences that, no matter how hard I tried, I never would have been able to plan myself. That's because the universe has way bigger plans for you than you have for yourself.

Anytime you feel the need to control the how, think of a series of events in your life that seemed insignificant at the time, yet ended up leading to something magical. Remember, you could have never planned all of those seemingly meaningless coincidences yourself, and those coincidences totally transformed your life. Whenever you try to control the how, you end up self-sabotaging because there's no space for the universe to work its magic. If you really care about those big dreams and you truly believe your success is inevitable, there's no need to hold onto the how.

Another great strategy for letting go of the how is thinking back on the times where you thought you wanted one thing, but the universe decided to give you something even better. I remember when I was applying to colleges. All I wanted was to be accepted to Cornell University. When I was rejected, I was heartbroken. Little did I know, a few months later, I would be accepted to Georgetown on almost a full scholarship.

Georgetown proved to be four of the best years of my life. During my time at Georgetown I started my first business, made lifelong friends, and even traveled the world. I can't imagine my life without Georgetown and, looking back, I am truly so thankful for that Cornell rejection. Remember, the universe always has big plans for you, often times even bigger than the ones you have for you!

You now have all of the tools you need to create the life and business you've been dreaming of throughout this book. This potential has always been inside of you. All you needed was to make a few shifts to let go of the fears, limiting beliefs, and bad habits that have been holding you back. The world is your oyster. I know you are going to live a life that's even more amazing than you ever thought was possible. All you need to do is stop getting in your own way!

HOW TO APPLY THIS CHAPTER TO YOUR LIFE TODAY:

1. Practice manifestation by starting with something small, like a cup of coffee or a front row parking spot.
2. Think about a time in your life when you couldn't have possibly controlled all the small coincidences that resulted in something amazing.
3. Believe your success is inevitable and let go of the rest.

WORKS REFERENCED

———

INTRODUCTION

Eker, T. (2016). Secrets of the millionaire mind. Hove: Joosr Ltd.

Nawbo.org. (2019). Women Business Owner Statistics | NAWBO. [online] Available at: https://www.nawbo.org/resources/women-business-owner-statistics [Accessed 1 Nov. 2019].

Speakola. (2019). Jim Carrey: 'Life doesn't happen to you, it happens for you', Maharishi University of Management, 2014 — Speakola. [online] Available at: https://speakola.com/grad/jim-carrey-maharishi-2014 [Accessed 1 Nov. 2019].

CHAPTER 1

Covey, S. (1999). The 7 habits of highly effective people. London: Simon & Schuster.

David R Hamilton PhD. (2019). David R Hamilton PhD | Does your brain distinguish real from imaginary?David R Hamilton PhD. [online] Available at: https://drdavidhamilton.com/does-your-brain-distinguish-real-from-imaginary/ [Accessed 1 Nov. 2019].

Goodreads.com. (2019). A quote by Henry Ford. [online] Available at: https://www.goodreads.com/quotes/978-whether-you-think-you-can-or-you-think-you-can-t--you-re [Accessed 1 Nov. 2019].

Inc.com. (2019). This Is the Way You Need to Write Down Your Goals for Faster Success. [online] Available at: https://www.inc.com/peter-economy/this-is-way-you-need-to-write-down-your-goals-for-faster-success.html [Accessed 1 Nov. 2019].

Keller, G. and Papasan, J. (2013). The ONE THING: The Surprisingly Simple Truth Behind Extraordinary Results. Bard Press.

CHAPTER 2

Eker, T. (2016). Secrets of the millionaire mind. Hove: Joosr Ltd.

Haefner, J. (2019). Mental Rehearsal & Psychology Aspects of Basketball – Visualization. [online] Breakthroughbasketball.com. Available at: https://www.breakthroughbasketball.com/mental/visualization.html [Accessed 1 Nov. 2019].

Hoffman, J. (2019). Why Jim Carrey Wrote Himself a $10-Million Check Before He Had $10 Million. [online] Medium. Available at: https://medium.com/@socialmediajosh/why-jim-carrey-wrote-himself-a-10-million-check-before-he-had-10-million-3618090c9e [Accessed 1 Nov. 2019].

Sasson, R. (2019). How Many Thoughts Does Your Mind Think in One Hour?. [online] Successconsciousness.com. Available at: https://www.successconsciousness.com/blog/inner-peace/how-many-thoughts-does-your-mind-think-in-one-hour/ [Accessed 1 Nov. 2019].

Sparks, S. (2019). The Power of Visualization in Sports and in Life – The Good Men Project. [online] The Good Men Project. Available at: https://goodmenproject.com/featured-content/the-power-of-visualisation-in-sports-and-in-life-s1s/ [Accessed 1 Nov. 2019].

CHAPTER 3

Motivation, F. (2019). Rich Dad Poor Dad Mastermind Robert Kiyosaki Quotes For Success. [online] Fearless Motivation – Motivational Videos & Music. Available at: https://www.fearlessmotivation.com/2018/06/20/rich-dad-poor-dad-robert-kiyosaki-quotes/ [Accessed 1 Nov. 2019].

Ranker. (2019). The Best Mildred Lisette Norman Quotes. [online] Available at: https://www.ranker.com/list/a-list-of-famous-mildred-lisette-norman-quotes/reference [Accessed 1 Nov. 2019].

CHAPTER 4

Covey, S. (1999). The 7 habits of highly effective people. London: Simon & Schuster.

CHAPTER 5

Bernstein, G. (2016). The Universe Has Your Back. [Place of publication not identified]: Hay House.

Famous Entrepreneurs. (2019). Robert Kiyosaki | Biography, Pictures and Facts. [online] Available at: https://www.famous-entrepreneurs.com/robert-kiyosaki [Accessed 1 Nov. 2019].

Improve Conversation. (2019). Everything takes longer than you think. – Improve Conversation. [online] Available at: https://improveconversation.com/2019/05/17/everything-takes-longer-than-you-think/ [Accessed 1 Nov. 2019].

Inc.com. (2019). How Walt Disney, Oprah Winfrey, and 19 Other Successful People Rebounded After Getting Fired. [online] Available at: https://www.inc.com/business-insider/21-successful-people-who-rebounded-after-getting-fired.html [Accessed 1 Nov. 2019].

CHAPTER 6

BrainyQuote. (2019). Arthur Ashe Quotes. [online] Available at: https://www.brainyquote.com/quotes/arthur_ashe_371527 [Accessed 1 Nov. 2019].

Gale, P. (2013). Your network is your net worth. Atria Books.

Medium. (2019). You Are The Average Of The Five People You Spend The Most Time With. [online] Available at: https://medium.com/the-polymath-project/you-are-the-average-of-the-five-people-you-spend-the-most-time-with-a2ea32d08c72 [Accessed 1 Nov. 2019].

Recruiter. (2019). To Be Successful, Burn Your Boats. [online] Available at: https://www.recruiter.com/i/to-be-successful-burn-your-boats/ [Accessed 1 Nov. 2019].

CHAPTER 7

Bernstein, G. (2016). The Universe Has Your Back. [Place of publication not identified]: Hay House.

Goodreads.com. (2019). A quote by Marie Forleo. [online] Available at: https://www.goodreads.com/quotes/9023778-clarity-comes-from-action-not-thought [Accessed 1 Nov. 2019].

Goodreads.com. (2019). A quote from Lean In. [online] Available at: https://www.goodreads.com/quotes/749769-done-is-better-than-perfect [Accessed 1 Nov. 2019].

Zenkina, K. (2019). Manifestation Babe.

CHAPTER 8

Boyd, D. (2019). Workplace Stress – The American Institute of Stress. [online] The American Institute of Stress. Available at: https://www.stress.org/workplace-stress [Accessed 3 Nov. 2019].

BrainyQuote. (2019). Arthur Ashe Quotes. [online] Available at: https://www.brainyquote.com/quotes/arthur_ashe_371527 [Accessed 1 Nov. 2019].

BrainyQuote. (2019). Wayne Dyer Quotes. [online] Available at: https://www.brainyquote.com/quotes/wayne_dyer_154410 [Accessed 3 Nov. 2019].

Goodreads.com. (2019). A quote by Tim Notke. [online] Available at: https://www.goodreads.com/quotes/3217324-hard-work-beats-talent-when-talent-doesn-t-work-hard [Accessed 3 Nov. 2019].

Kabir Sehgal, C. (2019). Stanford professor: Working this many hours a week is basically pointless. Here's how to get more done—by doing less. [online] CNBC. Available at: https://www.cnbc.com/2019/03/20/stanford-study-longer-hours-doesnt-make-you-more-productive-heres-how-to-get-more-done-by-doing-less.html [Accessed 3 Nov. 2019].

Lifehack. (2019). How to Use Parkinson's Law to Your Advantage. [online] Available at: https://www.lifehack.org/articles/featured/how-to-use-parkinsons-law-to-your-advantage.html [Accessed 3 Nov. 2019].

RescueTime Blog. (2019). The Planning Fallacy: Why We Assume We Have More Time Than We Do. [online] Available at: https://blog.rescuetime.com/planning-fallacy/ [Accessed 3 Nov. 2019].

Wedmore, J. (2019). The Mind Your Business Podcast.

CHAPTER 9

Business Insider. (2019). How To Become So Good They Can't Ignore You. [online] Available at: https://www.businessinsider.com/become-so-good-they-cant-ignore-you-2014-7 [Accessed 4 Nov. 2019].

Goodreads.com. (2019). A quote by Johnny Depp. [online] Available at: https://www.goodreads.com/quotes/7273297-one-day-the-people-that-didn-t-believe-in-you-will [Accessed 4 Nov. 2019].

Goodreads.com. (2019). A quote by Zig Ziglar. [online] Available at: https://www.goodreads.com/quotes/7649223-don-t-let-someone-who-gave-up-on-their-dreams-talk [Accessed 4 Nov. 2019].

ACKNOWLEDGEMENTS

———

I am immensely grateful for each and every person who played a role in helping make Stop Getting in Your Own Way a reality. First and foremost, I'd like to thank my family, for supporting me in publishing this book as well as through every step of my business journey. Mom and dad, thank you for teaching me to never give up and believing in me even when I didn't believe in myself. Richie, thank you for being my best friend, teammate and number one fan. Rachel, Christina, Kevin, Keith and Bradley, thank you for always cheering me on every step of the way.

Thank you to my friends for your endless support in this book and all my ventures. Thank you to my mentors and coaches for teaching me many of the lessons I teach in this book. I wouldn't be where I am today without your support and guidance.

To Eric Koester, thank you for always pushing me to be the best version of myself. I truly don't know where I would be on this journey without you. Thank you to Brian Bies, Bailee Noella, Leila Summers, Amanda Brown, Victoria Lei, Davor Dramikanin, Gjorgji Pejkovsk and the whole team at New Degree Press for helping make this book a reality.

Finally thank you to everyone who pre-ordered my book to help make publishing possible, I am sincerely grateful for all of your support and generosity.

University of Virginia Inter-Sorority Council	Casey Algeo
	Kamie Lehmann
Chris Ritchie	Rachel Douglas
Penn State Brandywine Boost	Christina Geraghty
Richard Gallo	Goodwin Chan
Adrienne Gallo	Cindy Celine
Theresa DiGregorio	Eric Koester
John DiGregorio	Christina Orlando
The Uncommon Individual Foundation	Michael Fabrizio
	Noreen Fabrizio
Rosemary Christian	Jasmine Williams
Kimberly Keane	Allison Sharkey
Katie Pijanowski	Melynda Link

Renee Prince

Audrey O'Neill

Elaine Turso

Mary Ellen Kane

Haley Hoffman Smith

Maddie Catts

Lauren Micchelli

Shannon Minnis

Emma Eklin

Angela Wilson

Maddie Niebanck

Elaine Mercedes Mendoza

Karen Spadaro

Allison Alt

Danielle Berardi

Trish Kovach

John Laprise

Rebecca Cassidy

Abby Wellner

Gail Davis

Linda McElvenny

Sophia Peyton

Samantha Leonard

Made in the USA
Middletown, DE
09 July 2021

43908191R00091